SQUADRO

No. 21

The Boeing
Fortress Mk II & Mk III

Phil H. Listemann

ISBN: 979-1096490-10-3

Copyright
© 2017 Philedition - Phil Listemann

Colour profiles: Gaetan Marie/Bravo Bravo Aviation

All right reserved. No part of this book may be reproduced, stored in a retrieval system or transmitted in any form by any means, electronic, mechanical, photocopying, recording or otherwise, without prior permission of the author.

Contributors & Acknowledgments:
Hugh Halliday, Andrew Thomas and special thanks to Robert M Stitt.

GLOSSARY OF TERMS

PERSONEL :
(AUS)/RAF: Australian serving in the RAF
(BEL)/RAF: Belgian serving in the RAF
(CAN)/RAF: Canadian serving in the RAF
(CZ)/RAF: Czechoslovak serving in the RAF
(NFL)/RAF: Newfoundlander serving in the RAF
(NL)/RAF: Dutch serving in the RAF
(NZ)/RAF: New Zealander serving in the RAF
(POL)/RAF: Pole serving in the RAF
(RHO)/RAF: Rhodesian serving in the RAF
(SA)/RAF: South African serving in the RAF
(US)/RAF - RCAF : American serving in the RAF or RCAF

RANKS
G/C : Group Captain
W/C : Wing Commander
S/L : Squadron Leader
F/L : Flight Lieutenant
F/O : Flying Officer
P/O : Pilot Officer
W/O : Warrant Officer
F/Sgt : Flight Sergeant
Sgt : Sergeant
Cpl : Corporal
LAC : Leading Aircraftman

OTHER
ATA: Air Transport Auxiliary
CO : Commander
DFC : Distinguished Flying Cross
DFM : Distinguished Flying Medal
DSO : Distinguished Service Order
Eva. : Evaded
ORB : Operational Record Book
OTU : Operational Training Unit
PoW : Prisoner of War
PAF: Polish Air Force
RAF : Royal Air Force
RAAF : Royal Australian Air Force
RCAF : Royal Canadian Air Force
RNZAF : Royal New Zealand Air Force
SAAF : South African Air Force
s/d: Shot down
Sqn : Squadron
† : Killed

THE FORTRESS MK II & MK III

The Fortress Mk.II and Mk.III were the equivalent of the USAAF's B-17E/F and G. The Fortress Mk.I was the B-17C as featured in 'SQUADRONS! No. 4'. The Fortress Mk.I was only used in small numbers (20), but, for the British, it was the first step leading to the large scale introduction of the Fortress to Bomber Command. The first Lend-Lease order had already been placed in 1941 for 300 B-17F model Fortresses with the following serials: FA675-FA823 (149) and FH467-FH617 (151). They were to be called the Fortress Mk.II. Found to be unsatisfactory for night and day bombing, the RAF eventually decided against using the Fortress in Bomber Command and the order for the 300 aircraft was cancelled. However, in the meantime, trials of the Fortress in Coastal Command proved satisfactory and, as this Command was looking for long-range land-based patrol aircraft, the Fortress was requested to equip three squadrons plus reserves. Therefore, a small quantity was diverted from US contracts, but, initially, no B-17Fs could be delivered to the RAF as the USAAF had reserved the latest variant for its own units that were now at war. Some B-17Es were offered instead. Being slightly different to the B-17F, they became the Fortress IIA in RAF service. Thirty were delivered between April and July 1942 (**FK184-FK213**) and another batch of 54 should have followed (FL449-FL502). Here too, however, the Americans, needing those Fortresses for training purposes Stateside, only delivered fifteen up to July 1942 (**FL449-FL460** and **FL462-FL464**). That situation jeopardised the formation of the three proposed Fortress squadrons. However, at the end of June 1942, arrangements were made with the Americans who promised to deliver more aircraft. They did, but the deliveries were late and took place between November 1942 and February 1943. In all, nineteen B-17Fs were released and were allocated the serials **FA695-FA713**, partially using the serials given to the original order of 300 aircraft. The Fortresses in this batch became Fortress Mk IIs. The USAAF, being involved in strategic bombing over the Continent from the UK or North Africa, and sustaining heavy losses, could not deliver more Fortresses to the British who subsequently had to revise their plans for the type. From three squadrons, only two remained operational on the Fortress in 1943 with No. 59 Squadron converting to the Liberator in March 1943. At the end of 1943, with production increasing, the Americans let the British know they could make Fortresses of the latest type, the B-17G, available from early 1944 onwards. Sixty were requested as Fortress Mk IIIs and the serials allocated were **HB761-HB820**. Thirty-eight were delivered between March and June 1944, with the balance (HB761, HB764, HB766, HB770-HB771, HB773, HB777, HB781, HB783, HB794, HB797-HB798, HB804) being diverted to the USAAF when the aircraft reached the UK after an exchange with the 8th Air Force, for roughly the same number of aircraft already in service, was made, nine more (HB806 to HB814) were not delivered and issued to the USAAF in Europe. Further requests for 35 more (**KH993-KJ127**) followed, but the first five were never delivered to the RAF. These deliveries took place between July 1944 and February 1945. This batch was followed by eight more in March and April 1945 (**KL830-KL837**). Those deliveries arrived too late and, with the better range of the Liberator and its greater availability from the US factories, the RAF had decided not to expand its number of Fortress squadrons. By the summer 1944, only one Coastal Command squadron, 220, was still flying the Fortress and this would remain the case until almost the end of the war. At that time there were enough examples of the Fortress II or IIA on hand and, consequently, only a handful of Fortress IIIs would be used for General Reconnaissance duties.

So by the end of 1944 the RAF had plenty of unused B-17s at its depots when they had been in high demand two years earlier. However, the Fortress found a new role early in 1944 when it was selected to fly electronic countermeasures operations with Bomber Command. At the time, the RAF was short of Fortresses and, in anticipation of future deliveries of the Fortress Mk.III, it obtained the transfer of fourteen more or less war-weary B-17Fs from the 8th Air Force (see above). These Fortresses received the serials **SR376-SR389** and logically became the Fortress Mk.II. They are sometimes referred to as being Fortress IIAs, but their respective movement cards give no doubt as to the denomination given to the B-17F. Later on, the USAAF would divert thirteen B-17Gs upon arrival in England which

Boeing Fortress Mk.II FA706 seen while conducted astrodome trials at the A&AEE. Arriving in the UK by air on 07.11.42, it was initially sent to the A&AEE at the end of December. When the trials were completed it was made available for operational squadrons and eventually served with 220 Sqn from April 1943 until August 1944 when it was lost in an accident.

Boeing Fortress IIA FK187 taken shortly after its arrival in the UK 08.04.42. It was never issued to an operational squadron and served for type trials. When these were completed, it was sent for overhaul at Scottish Aviation in November 1943 and then stored in June 1944. It then served at various Coastal Command stations, like Thornaby or Gosport, between September 1944 and February 1945. Returned to Scottish Aviation in February, apparently for modifications, the work was eventually suspended on 12 June 1945 with the end of the war and the aircraft was finally struck off charge on 7 July.

Fortress IIA FK187 seen during a test flight. As it was used for type trials, it was considered a prototype, hence the 'P' painted on the fuselage. Note that the USAAF serial 41-25196 has been crudely overpainted.

explains why thirteen Fortress IIIs were cut from the 'HB' batch. Those second-hand Fortress IIs were replaced from the summer of 1944 onwards by Fortress IIIs, and by early 1945 the III was the only operational mark in Bomber Command. In March and April, the second electronic countermeasures squadron, No. 223, equipped with second-hand Liberators, began its conversion to the Fortress and the squadron would fly its final operations of the war on the type. In all, the RAF took charge of 45 Fortress IIAs (B-17E), 33 Fortress IIs (B-17F) and 85 Fortress IIIs (B-17G) of which 30, 19 and 60 respectively are still in RAF hand at VE-Day. They soldiered on until the end of the war, mainly in a role that was never in the spotlight, but that doesn't mean that what they did was insignificant: 2,600 sorties and 26,445 hours of patrols with twelve U-boats sunk (two being shared) for the Coastal Command and close to 1,300 sorties for the Bomber Command.

The Fortresses soon disappeared from the RAF inventory, the first being the aircraft under repairs or in the process of being modified, like FK188 and FK187, both struck off charge, while the others eventually went into storage where they awaited their fate. The last withdrawal from flying units took place at the end of spring 1946. As they were in excess of the USAAF's surplus, they were not sent back to the USA and were scrapped in England. By the autumn of 1947, no Fortresses remained in the RAF's inventory. Most were struck off charge in March 1947, but FA709, KJ127 and KL832 survived until 15 September.

A Fortress Mk.III, HB773, as it was delivered by Boeing in 1944 in natural metal finish. HB773 was built as 42-97110 and this serial has been overpainted. The aircraft is probably seen at Dorval in February 1944 and was returned to the USAAF in exchange for transfers that had taken place in the UK. Of the other thirteen aircraft involved in the 'deal', HB761 was issued to an operational bomb group in the 8th AF along with all the others but HB766, HB773 and HB781 which returned to the US. HB771 was converted to a C-108.

RAF SERIALS CORRESPONDING TO USAAF SERIALS
* not delivered

RAF	USAAF	Built as	RAF	USAAF	Built as
FA695:	42-24594	B-17F-27-BO	**FL455:**	41-9225	B-17E-BO
FA696:	42-24595	B-17F-27-BO	**FL456:**	41-9230	B-17E-BO
FA697:	42-24596	B-17F-27-BO	**FL457:**	41-9229	B-17E-BO
FA698:	42-24597	B-17F-27-BO	**FL458:**	41-9197	B-17E-BO
FA699:	42-24598	B-17F-27-BO	**FL459:**	41-9241	B-17E-BO
FA700:	42-24599	B-17F-27-BO	**FL460:**	41-9201	B-17E-BO
FA701:	42-5065	B-17F-30-BO	***FL461:****	*41-9234*	*B-17E-BO*
FA702:	42-5066	B-17F-30-BO	**FL462:**	41-9239	B-17E-BO
FA703:	42-5067	B-17F-30-BO	**FL463:**	41-9236	B-17E-BO
FA704:	42-5073	B-17F-30-BO	**FL464:**	41-9238	B-17E-BO
FA705:	42-5074	B-17F-30-BO	***HB761:****	*42-97098*	*B-17G-40-BO*
FA706:	42-5075	B-17F-30-BO	**HB762:**	42-97099	B-17G-40-BO
FA707:	42-5234	B-17F-40-BO	**HB763:**	42-97100	B-17G-40-BO
FA708:	42-5235	B-17F-40-BO	***HB764:****	*42-97101*	*B-17G-40-BO*
FA709:	42-5236	B-17F-40-BO	**HB765:**	42-97102	B-17G-40-BO
FA710:	42-5237	B-17F-40-BO	***HB766:****	*42-97103*	*B-17G-40-BO*
FA711:	42-5238	B-17F-40-BO	**HB767:**	42-97104	B-17G-40-BO
FA712:	42-5239	B-17F-40-BO	**HB768:**	42-97105	B-17G-40-BO
FA713:	42-5240	B-17F-40-BO	**HB769:**	42-97106	B-17G-40-BO
FK184:	41-2513	B-17E-BO	***HB770:****	*42-97107*	*B-17G-40-BO*
FK185:	41-2514	B-17E-BO	**HB771:**	42-97108	B-17G-40-BO
FK186:	41-2515	B-17E-BO	**HB772:**	42-97109	B-17G-40-BO
FK187:	41-2516	B-17E-BO	***HB773:****	*42-97110*	*B-17G-40-BO*
FK188:	41-2517	B-17E-BO	**HB774:**	42-97111	B-17G-40-BO
FK189:	41-2518	B-17E-BO	**HB775:**	42-97112	B-17G-40-BO
FK190:	41-2519	B-17E-BO	**HB776:**	42-97113	B-17G-40-BO
FK191:	41-2522	B-17E-BO	***HB777:****	*42-97114*	*B-17G-40-BO*
FK192:	41-2615	B-17E-BO	**HB778:**	42-97115	B-17G-40-BO
FK193:	41-2526	B-17E-BO	**HB779:**	42-97116	B-17G-40-BO
FK194:	41-2620	B-17E-BO	**HB780:**	42-97117	B-17G-40-BO
FK195:	41-2608	B-17E-BO	***HB781:****	*42-97118*	*B-17G-40-BO*
FK196:	41-2623	B-17E-BO	**HB782:**	42-97119	B-17G-40-BO
FK197:	41-2625	B-17E-BO	***HB783:****	*42-102434*	*B-17G-50-BO*
FK198:	41-2622	B-17E-BO	***HB784:****	*42-102435*	*B-17G-50-BO*
FK199:	41-2614	B-17E-BO	**HB785:**	42-102436	B-17G-50-BO
FK200:	41-2619	B-17E-BO	**HB786:**	42-102437	B-17G-50-BO
FK201:	41-2618	B-17E-BO	**HB787:**	42-102438	B-17G-50-BO
FK202:	41-9138	B-17E-BO	**HB788:**	42-102439	B-17G-50-BO
FK203:	41-9195	B-17E-BO	**HB789:**	42-102940	B-17G-60-BO
FK204:	41-9136	B-17E-BO	**HB790:**	42-102941	B-17G-60-BO
FK205:	41-9135	B-17E-BO	**HB791:**	42-98021	B-17G-40-VE
FK206:	41-9202	B-17E-BO	**HB792:**	42-98022	B-17G-40-VE
FK207:	41-9204	B-17E-BO	**HB793:**	42-98023	B-17G-40-VE
FK208:	41-9198	B-17E-BO	***HB794:****	*42-98024*	*B-17G-40-VE*
FK209:	41-9203	B-17E-BO	**HB795:**	42-98025	B-17G-40-VE
FK210:	41-9200	B-17E-BO	**HB796:**	42-98026	B-17G-40-VE
FK211:	41-9199	B-17E-BO	***HB797:****	*42-98027*	*B-17G-40-VE*
FK212:	41-9237	B-17E-BO	***HB798:****	*42-98028*	*B-17G-40-VE*
FK213:	41-3232	B-17E-BO	**HB799:**	42-98029	B-17G-40-VE
FL449:	41-9243	B-17E-BO	**HB800:**	42-98030	B-17G-40-VE
FL450:	41-9240	B-17E-BO	**HB801:**	42-98031	B-17G-40-VE
FL451:	41-9231	B-17E-BO	**HB802:**	42-98032	B-17G-40-VE
FL452:	41-9242	B-17E-BO	**HB803:**	42-98033	B-17G-40-VE
FL453:	41-9228	B-17E-BO	***HB804:****	*42-98034*	*B-17G-40-VE*
FL454:	41-9245	B-17E-BO	**HB805:**	42-98035	B-17G-40-VE

RAF	USAAF	Built as	RAF	USAAF	Built as
HB806:*	44-8073	B-17G-45-VE	**KJ118:**	44-8621	B-17G-75-VE
HB807:*	44-8074	B-17G-45-VE	**KJ119:**	44-8622	B-17G-75-VE
HB808:*	44-8075	B-17G-45-VE	**KJ120:**	44-8623	B-17G-75-VE
HB809:*	44-8076	B-17G-45-VE	**KJ121:**	44-8624	B-17G-75-VE
HB810:*	44-8077	B-17G-45-VE	**KJ122:**	44-8625	B-17G-75-VE
HB811:*	44-8078	B-17G-45-VE	**KJ123:**	44-8626	B-17G-75-VE
HB812:*	44-8079	B-17G-45-VE	**KJ124:**	44-8627	B-17G-75-VE
HB813:*	44-8080	B-17G-45-VE	**KJ125:**	44-8628	B-17G-75-VE
HB814:*	44-8081	B-17G-45-VE	**KJ126:**	44-8861	B-17G-85-VE
HB815:	44-8082	B-17G-45-VE	**KJ127:**	44-8862	B-17G-85-VE
HB816:	44-8083	B-17G-45-VE	**KL830:**	44-8863	B-17G-85-VE
HB817:	44-8084	B-17G-45-VE	**KL831:**	44-8864	B-17G-85-VE
HB818:	44-8085	B-17G-45-VE	**KL832:**	44-8865	B-17G-85-VE
HB819:	44-8086	B-17G-45-VE	**KL833:**	44-8966	B-17G-90-VE
HB820:	44-8087	B-17G-45-VE	**KL834:**	44-8967	B-17G-90-VE
KH998:	44-8240	B-17G-55-VE	**KL835:**	44-8968	B-17G-90-VE
KH999:	44-8241	B-17G-55-VE	**KL836:**	44-8969	B-17G-90-VE
KJ100:	44-8442	B-17G-55-VE	**KL837:**	44-8970	B-17G-90-VE
KJ101:	44-8243	B-17G-55-VE	**SR376:**	42-3177	B-17F-30-DL
KJ102:	44-8244	B-17G-55-VE	**SR377:**	42-30014	B-17F-80-BO
KJ103:	44-8336	B-17G-60-VE	**SR378:**	42-30241	B-17F-95-BO
KJ104:	44-8337	B-17G-60-VE	**SR379:**	42-30451	B-17F-105-BO
KJ105:	44-8338	B-17G-60-VE	**SR380:**	42-30639	B-17F-115-BO
KJ106:	44-8339	B-17G-60-VE	**SR381:**	42-30773	B-17F-120-BO
KJ107:	44-8340	B-17G-60-VE	**SR382:**	42-30809	B-17F-120-BO
KJ108:	44-8341	B-17G-60-VE	**SR383:**	42-30812	B-17F-120-BO
KJ109:	44-8342	B-17G-60-VE	**SR384:**	42-30970	B-17F-130-BO
KJ110:	44-8343	B-17G-60-VE	**SR385:**	42-30986	B-17F-130-BO
KJ111:	44-8534	B-17G-70-VE	**SR386:**	**	
KJ112:	44-8535	B-17G-70-VE	**SR387:**	42-31027	B-17F-130-BO
KJ113:	44-8536	B-17G-70-VE	**SR388:**	42-31031	B-17F-130-BO
KJ114:	44-8537	B-17G-70-VE	**SR389:**	42-3169***	B-17F-35-DL
KJ115:	44-8538	B-17G-70-VE	*Not delivered		
KJ116:	44-8619	B-17G-75-VE	**possibly 42-31012.		
KJ117:	44-8620	B-17G-75-VE	*** to be confirmed as SR389 is also given as formerly 42-3218.		

Fortress HB766 seen just after its transfer back to the US which took place on 22 March 1944 shortly after its arrival in the UK. Therefore, the former US serial deleted in the US (see p5) was painted back on the tail but it was not the good one, 42-97109 corresponding normally to HB772 which was maintained in the RAF. It is not sure that this error was rectified for 42-97103 as the aircraft seems to have been never issued to any 8th AF unit.

July 1942
April 1945

U-boat victories - confirmed or probable claims: 4.16
Hours of patrol flown: 17,090

First operational sortie: 24.07.42
Last operational sortie: 26.04.45

Number of sorties: 1,646
Total aircraft written-off: 11
Aircraft lost on operations: 8
Aircraft lost in accidents: 3

Squadron code letters:

NR (up to end 1942), 2 (Oct 43 - Apr 44), ZZ (from Apr 44)

Commanding Officers

W/C Richard T.F. Gates	RAF No. 37064	RAF	...	05.09.42
W/C Patrick E. Hadow (†)	RAF No. 36026	RAF	05.09.42	25.12.43
W/C James M.N. Pike	RAF No. 33200	RAF	01.01.44	29.11.44
W/C Benedict O. Dias	RAF No. 39185	RAF	29.11.44	...

SQUADRON USAGE

The introduction of the Fortress II was a logical step for the squadron as it had conducted the trials on the Fortress for Coastal Command in the first half of 1942 (see SQUADRONS! No. 4). The squadron was operating from Ballykelly, near Londonderry in Northern Ireland, and was still under the command of W/C R.T.F. Gates. In July, it received eleven Fortress Mk.IIs (FK185, FK186, FK193, FK196, FK199, FK200, FK203, FK204, FK206, FK207 and FK212) and the first sortie, a ten-hour convoy escort, was carried out on the 24th by FK207/J flown by S/L William. That was the operational debut of the Fortress Mk.II. Three days later, the Fortress Mk.I performed its final sorties, leaving its successor to continue the job. Nine more sorties were flown before the end of July and all were uneventful. Operational activity increased in August with sixty sorties flown, representing more than 450 hours of flight, but bad luck hit the squadron with the loss of two aircraft. On 10 August, returning from a convoy escort, FK207/J, the aircraft that flew the first Mk.II patrol, crashed at Nutts Corner when caught by bad weather. All of the six crewmembers on board were killed. At the same time the CO (W/C Gates), who had taken off early that day, had also been caught by the weather on the same leg back to base and made contact with 15 Group flying control. Over the next few hours, a series of factors combined so the crew was unable to find any airfield on which to land. When the Fortress was about to run out of fuel, at about 01.00, the captain gave the order to abandon the aircraft. All of the crewmembers landed safety by parachute while the Fortress crashed a couple of minutes later near Acklington in Northumberland. It wasn't a good start for the Fortress especially since all the crews who returned to base in August did so with nothing to report.

At the beginning of September, W/C Gates relinquished command to W/C P.E. Hadow. That month, the squadron made its first attack with depth charges when,

Wing Commander Patrick Hadow took over 220 Sqn in September 1942 until he lost his life on 25 December 1943 while returning to the Azores from a meeting in the UK.

Fortress FK186 was one the first Fortress IIs to join 220 Sqn in July 1942. It was coded 'S'. In August 1943, it was passed on to 206 Sqn as 'X' before returning to 220 in March 1944 and continuing to fly as 'X'. Sent to Scottish Aviation in mid-December 1944 to be overhauled, the work was actually never completed and the aircraft was therefore declared 'Cat E' on 29 May and officially struck off charge on 13.06.45.

while on a sweep on the 19th, the crew of FK186/S (P/O Houghton) sighted a bubble patch rising from a submerged source a few feet below the surface. The Fortress attacked from fifty feet, but no result was visible as the four depth charges overshot. The rear gunner fired with his two 0.50 MGs, but, again, no results were observed. However, two small pieces of driftwood were seen over 300 yards away. The Fortress remained in vicinity for about half an hour and eventually an oil track, measuring four miles long, was detected and ceased one mile from the scene of the attack. A flame float was dropped to try to ignite the oil patches, but that failed. No claim was made. Other than this attack, September was uneventful over the 500 hours of patrols carried out. More than 550 hours were flown in October and about 625 in November, the best figure so far despite the bad weather prevailing over the North Atlantic, but those two months would remain quiet as far as the U-boat hunt was concerned. With weather deteriorating in December, operational activity was almost cut by half, so the chances to encounter a U-Boat diminished and, as with the previous months, 'nothing to report' became the standard comment on return from patrol.

The year 1943 started as 1942 ended with a total absence of U-boat encounters. Even though the weather prevented much operational flying, the whole situation was frustrating since the sister squadron, 206, had already opened its score against the U-boats. A new era began in February, however. On the 3rd, Fortress FL456/N (P/O Kenneth Ramsden) was flying a daytime sweep for a convoy when the crew spotted a U-boat at four miles, through a gap in the clouds, while 29 miles from the convoy. Ramsden descended from his patrol altitude (3000 feet) and positioned the aircraft with the sun behind him to attack from fifty feet with all seven depth charges. The crew saw the detonations produce some oil, seen in the centre of a patch of disturbed water immediately after the attack, but that quickly dispersed in the rough water. It was not enough to declare the target as sunk, so it was claimed as damaged, but the U-Boat, U-265, was actually sunk as confirmed after the war in September 1945. Another attack was made four days later by P/O G.P. Roberson in FL459/J. While sweeping off a convoy, a U-Boat was seen running on the surface a few miles away. Roberson climbed into cloud and approached through a squall to ensure a surprise attack. He released his depth charges from fifty feet while the submarine's conning tower was still partially above the surface. The fourth and fifth depth charges straddled the U-boat as it submerged very slowly. This was fatal for U-624. It was the first official U-Boat sinking for the squadron since conversion to the Fortress. In mid-February, the squadron made a small move, being relocated to Aldergrove near Belfast.

Two U-Boat attacks were achieved in March. While flying a convoy escort patrol on 7 March, F/O William Knowles and crew in FL459/J spotted a submarine sailing at about twelve knots on the surface, two miles off the port bow. The pilot made an attack by diving at the U-Boat and delivered the depth charges from eighty feet while it was diving. U-641 was damaged, but survived. Flying Officer Knowles would also be responsible for the second attack that occurred on the 19th. Having taken off from Benbecula (the squadron moved to the Outer Hebrides on the 13th of that month), at 05.32, the crew spotted a U-Boat from 5000 feet, a few minutes befo-

Pilot Officer Kenneth Ramsden flew not only the first convoy escort performed by a Fortress I, but also made the first U-boat sinking using a Fortress II even though that feat would only be confirmed after the war (see text). (*Edward Ramsden via Robert M Stitt*)

re 10.00, sailing twelve miles off the bow. Knowles attacked with four depth charges dropped from eighty feet which exploded 100 feet ahead of the swirl made by the U-Boat (U-666). Diesel oil gushed to the surface and the U-Boat reappeared for fifty seconds then submerged and disappeared. Knowles made a second attack, with his last three depth charges, from bow to stern as the U-Boat was disappearing, but no results were observed. The U-Boat was damaged and it was later discovered that the captain made the decision to cut his patrol short and return to St-Nazaire. It was not a complete victory, but at least one U-Boat would be out of service for a little while.

In April, 41 sorties were carried out representing over 400 hours of flight during which three U-Boat attacks, all on 16 April, were made. First of all, two U-boats were seen and FL459/J (F/O G. Roberson) took care of one of them. The Fortress dived to attack the nearest one and the gunners fired short bursts that hit the conning tower. The attack was made from the port quarter, but the depth charges failed to release immediately. When five eventually did, they fell 200 yards beyond the swirl. The gunners took the opportunity to fire at the conning tower once more as they passed over it. The Fortress remained in the vicinity for the next seven minutes, but nothing happened so it returned to its patrol altitude of 4500 feet. A few minutes later, another submarine was seen twelve miles away and the attack was made from the port bow at 30° with the two remaining depth charges. The submarine submerged and one explosion was seen on the presumed track, the edge of the explosion touching the forward edge of the swirl. Nothing else happened and, having no more depth charges, Roberson asked to drop markers and returned to patrol for another three hours before landing at base. One hour and fifteen minutes later, it was the turn of FK201/T (F/L K. Tarwent) to spot a U-Boat while flying at 3500 feet. It was seen on surface eight miles away. The attack was made from the starboard bow, 5° off the U-Boat's track, and six depth charges were dropped. A light diesel oil patch 100 feet long was seen after the first circuit, but nothing else happened. Markers were dropped and the Fortress returned to patrol. Two hours later a periscope was sighted, but the U-Boat disappeared before another attack could be undertaken. After three months full of encounters, May was uneventful and only one attack was made in June. On the 6th, after four hours on patrol, a U-Boat was sighted on the surface by the crew of FL458/A (S/L H. Warren). It was attacked with three depth charges dropped spaced from 100 to 25 feet. The submarine turned sharply to starboard just before the attack and the depth charges fell 90° to the track, port to starboard. While flying above, the gunners fired about 1000 rounds of 0.5-in and 200 more from the 0.3-in in the nose. Warren made a second attack with the remaining charges, but they did not release. The U-Boat was seen to slowly submerge stern first. The U-Boat (U-450) was considered damaged. The squadron experienced a severe blow one week later, when Fortress FK212/V was posted missing from a patrol. Having taken-off from St Eval in Cornwall while on detachment to cover the south-west of England and the U-Boat transit routes in the Bay of Biscay, the radio operator transmitted a position at 20.15, but nothing else was heard. The Fortress had crossed paths with a Junkers Ju88C of 15./KG 40 and was shot down (*Leutnant* Lothar Wolff). All nine crewmen perished. By mid-1943, the opportunities to attack U-Boats in the North Atlantic were now almost non-existent. The detachment to St Eval became a temporary alternative, but the RAF was preparing for the big move to the Azores to cover the water between the Azores and the Bay of Biscay and from the Azores to beyond the Canary Islands to the west coast of Africa. After months of negotiation, Portugal and the Allies reached an agreement and the RAF was allowed to operate from the Azores at Lagens. The facilities and operating conditions at Lagens favoured the performance of the Fortress over the Liberator. The move took place from 20 October and up this date the squadron continued to operate from the UK. Between 1 July and 2 September, the last sortie from the UK, the squadron would carry out seventy sorties, representing 650 hours, with only one attack to report. On 3 August, Fortress 'F' (P/O J.D. Burnett) made an attack on a surfaced U-Boat in conjunction with a Hudson and a Catalina, but the U-Boat was able to escape thanks to a heavy rain cloud. Preparations and the move took place in September and into the first fortnight of October because some modifications had to be carried out. In particular, the squadron's aircraft had to be marked with a '2' to differentiate them from 206 Squadron's aircraft as that unit was also deployed to the Azores. It was the CO, W/C Patrick E. Hadow, who took the first Fortress, FK206/K, to the Azores, and the following day the first patrol was carried out with this aircraft and the crew of P/O James B. Taylor. The rest of the aircraft followed over the next few days, but were delayed because of bad weather, so FK206 was the only operational Fortress for a couple of days. Therefore, of course, operational activity for the month was limited. The squadron's debut was tragic, however, when Fortress FK202/L flown by S/L H.A.A. Webster did not return from a patrol that started with a take-off at 07.44 on the 24th. All of the crew was posted missing. Despite this, it was not long before the first U-Boat encounter. On 27 October, the crew of Fortress F (F/L Roderick P. Drummond), flying at 3500 feet, sighted a U-Boat on the surface from about three miles away. The attack was launched at once, but the Fortress was unable to lose height fast enough and by the time the aircraft was in position to deliver its attack, the U-Boat had submerged and left a smoke-float behind to disturb the accuracy of the attack. The only thing the Fortress could do was drop marine mar-

A colour image Fortress FK186 taken while flying over the sea. Note the light grey of the 'S' painted on the fuselage with the 'S' painted on the nose in accordance with the new regulations. The 'S', however, is still painted red. *(via Andrew Thomas)*

kers and then continue its patrol. For Drummond, while he missed this U-Boat, he would not miss the one encountered on 9 November. Two and a half hours into the patrol, and still dark, a U-Boat was sighted on the surface - almost directly under the Fortress. At the same time, the submarine's flak guns opened up with a heavy and fairly accurate barrage. The tail gunner responded by firing at the conning tower while the captain placed his aircraft in a good position to deliver four depth charges. This attack stopped the submarine and it was seen going down by the stern. A second attack with the three remaining depth charges sent U-707 to the bottom stern first. The crew later spotted a man in the water and dropped a dinghy and rations. Drummond was awarded an immediate DFC. This successful attack ended up being the only one in November, a month which saw the squadron's crews achieve about 780 hours of flight over 79 sorties. At the end of the month, an accident occurred during a training flight, but without causing any casualties. Fortress FA708, which had only been used for training duties thus far, took off to fly circuits and, ten minutes later, with two trainees, Lt Theodore W. Case of the USAAF and F/O William G. Cameron, as well as six others on board, the Fortress made its first approach. It began to undershoot close to touchdown, and the instructor, F/L Peter Roberson, didn't have time to correct before the Fortress hit a bank of earth short of the runway. The left undercarriage collapsed as the aircraft came to a stop. The aircraft was towed to the maintenance area where it seems no repairs were carried out for some reason and the Fortress was used for spare parts before being eventually struck off charge on 7 November 1944.

December saw the operational activity drop to 56 sorties and 570 hours, but the month saw the write-off of two Fortresses. FK206/K, crashed while on take-off for a major 800 hours inspection at Thorney Island, something that could not be undertaken at Lagens. The Fortress was seen to begin to turn to starboard before it plunged into the Atlantic with the loss of all on board. The squadron lost another Fortress that month, FA697/T, which crashed on return from patrol on the evening of the 19th. With very bad weather prevailing at Lagens, the captain, F/O John Ireland, who had had to face too many technical problems since he had taken off on patrol, having broken cloud, touched down mid-way along the runway. Having bounced once, Ireland told his co-pilot to raise the undercarriage to

A 220 Squadron's Fortress IIA being bombed up with depth charges. Note the Yagi Homing System Transmit Aerial located on the nose.

Issued to 220 Sqn in August 1942, this Fortress II FL459 would be coded 'J' until being transferred to 3502 SU at Gosport, in mid-December 1944, pending re-assignment which came in March when it was allocated to 519 Sqn, then 251 Sqn in July. It was struck off charge in December that year.

avoid going into the quarry at the end of the runway. The Fortress ended its landing run on its belly which signalled the end of its career. None on board was injured. It was a very bad run of events for the squadron as it lost its CO a few days later on board a Dakota (FD903 of 512 Squadron) which was posted missing. He was travelling to the UK for interviews with HQ Coastal Command on crew policies when the Dakota disappeared between Gibraltar and the UK. On 1 January 1944, W/C James M.N. Pike arrived by air to replace W/C Hadow. Pike was a very experienced Coastal Command pilot with a DSO (248 Squadron) and a DFC (203 Squadron). Otherwise, January was free of any action despite some U-Boats being seen. Likewise in February and in March, only one attack was made, when F/O Wilfred 'Pip' Travell dropped two depth charges on a previously spotted trail of oil left by a submerged and slow moving U-Boat. At that point, Travell was instructed to leave the area while the attack was taken over by surface vessels and Avengers of the USN. During the first three months of 1944, the squadron could lay claim to 240 sorties and 1500 hours of operational flying. That month, with the return of 206 Squadron to the UK, and their planned re-equipment with Liberators, some of that squadron's personnel and aircraft (FK186, FK198, FK213 and FL460) were transferred to 220 to bring its strength up to sixteen operational aircraft plus four spares. At the end of the month, another important event occurred when Fortress HB786, a Mk.III, arrived at Lagens on the 26th. HB786 would be one of the very few Mk IIIs assigned to a frontline Coastal Command squadron. This Fortress had been modified and was equipped with a Mk.X centimetric radar operating on a 10cm wavelength. However, HB786 would not have time to become operational as it suffered brake failure while taxiing and hit another Fortress (FK198). The latter aircraft was declared damaged beyond economical repair while HB786 was repaired and returned to service in September. By that time, two more Mk.IIIs had arrived, HB791 and HB792, and these three would constitute the only Mk.IIIs to serve with 220. The first sortie of a Fortress III took place on 6 July (HB791/T). On the operational side, April, May and June were rather uneventful despite over 3200 operational hours completed across 273 sorties. The squadron flew more than 1250 hours of operational patrols in July, resulting in just one U-boat sighting and attack at the end of the month. A radar contact was made by HB792/U, a Fortress Mk.III flown by Flying Officer F.H. Smith, after four hours of night patrol and, from the light of flares and the return flak, this proved to be a surfaced U-boat. Smith attacked immediately from fifty feet with six depth charges, spaced at 55 feet intervals with a ground speed of 200mph. Blue flashes were seen on both sides of the hull and the aircraft experienced severe shuddering as it passed overhead. Contact with the U-boat was then lost so a square search was begun, resulting in another radar contact being re-established one hour and forty minutes later. Smith attacked again with two depth charges at ninety degrees to the submarine's course. The U-boat replied with heavier flak from three guns and the Fortress was hit in the port elevator. It remained in the area, making sporadic radar contact with the U-boat, and by 06.00 was joined by FA699/K (F/L J.M. Ireland). The hunt was eventually given up, HB792/U landing at Lagens at 09.27 while Ireland's crew continued their patrol for a couple more hours. However, this attack could not come close to compensating for the loss of two Fortresses within a couple of hours two days previously. First, FA707/Z, while on a night anti-submarine patrol at 1200 feet, had its port outer engine begin to overspeed so the propeller was feathered. Within the next hour, both starboard engines suffered the same malady. Unable to maintain altitude on one engine, the captain, F/O Eric McIlwrick, had no choice but to ditch the Fortress. The crew was later rescued by a ship. Not long after, F/L Laurence H. Croft (RCAF) experienced a fire in the starboard outer engine of his FK189/Y while taking-off for a patrol. He shut down the engine and feathered the propeller prior to landing. The fire was extinguished, but the aircraft was considered beyond economical repair and written-off. Croft, in a run of bad luck, would also be responsible for the write-off of FA706/S. While taxiing the Fortress to the dispersal solo, he forgot to switch on the batteries and lost brake pressure. He overlooked the brake pressure warning light and taxied into an unidentified aircraft. The aircraft was too damaged to consider any repair. Otherwise, the squadron continued to carry out operational patrols day and night, but none led to any attacks even though some radar contacts were made. U-Boat activity had seriously decreased and the D-Day landings and the Battle of Normandy was probably one of the main causes as the U-Boats were assured of losing their bases in France so a total re-organisation was underway. There were U-Boats still in the area however, and the Fortress would enjoy some final successes over the German submarines. Indeed, on 26 September, Fortress FK191/P, with F/L A.F. Wallace, the squadron navigation officer, in command (the pilot was F/O Eric C.W. Fielder), was providing a daytime convoy escort north-west of the Azores when the crew intercepted a flash report from FK193/H (captained by F/L Carter) that a U-Boat sighting had been made. Soon in the area where a marker had been dropped, the two Fortresses were joined by FA701/F. Soon, however, FK193 and FA701 were asked to return to base and had to discontinue the hunt, leaving FK191 alone. After a couple of minutes a periscope was seen and Wallace gave the order to attack. Four depth charges were dropped from fifty feet, two of them entering the water on the port side of the U-Boat (U-871) and one on the starboard side. The fourth hung up. After the explosions, an oil patch formed which, fifty minutes later, was 700 yards by 1600 yards, amid which much debris was seen. The U-Boat was without doubt sunk.

In October, the most important event of the month from the squadron's point of view was the commencement of the conversion to the Leigh Light-equipped Liberator Mk.VI. The decision had been made in September and it was planned to send seven crews to St Davids for the conversion course with the return flight to Lagens being made in the new aircraft. The remainder of the squadron would go to

FL464 was another Fortress II and actually the last of this batch. It was initially issued to 59 Sqn as 'E', then was allocated to 220 in April 1943 as 'C'. The number '2' was added when 220 was based in the Azores. It was withdrawn from the squadron inventory on 17.11.44 and, as with FL459, went to 3502 SU temporarily. On 9 December it was issued to 519 Sqn, then 251 Sqn on 1 August. It was struck off charge on 22 December that year. *(via Robert M. Stitt)*

Fortress III HB791 had a similar career to HB792 (see next page) and is also seen without any camouflage markings. However, only the individual letter has been painted on suggesting that the photo was taken during the early weeks of its service with 220.

St Davids at a later stage. Accordingly, seven Fortresses (L, C, F, B, E, Q and O) left for St Davids on 12 October with captains F/L Huggins, F/O Fielder, F/L Cooke, F/L Carter, F/O Buchman, F/L Chisholm and F/L Croft respectively and their crews. Logically, with less crews and aircraft, operational activity diminished and only 700 hours were flown, over 59 sorties, that month during which one U-Boat contact and one radar contact were made, but without follow up attacks. In September, the figures had been 1243 hours over 103 sorties. In November, enemy U-Boat activity in the area covered by the Azores-based aircraft was practically nil. The squadron's operational activity was considerably reduced and only about 230 hours were flown in 26 sorties with no U-Boat sightings made. At the end of the month, W/C Pike was posted to HQ 16 Group and relinquished command to W/C B.O. Dias. Actually Pike had been detached RAF Thornaby and later RAF St David since September, the 220 having been under the temporary command of Squadron Leader R.G. English since then. The level of operational activity was maintained in December and, for the first time in about two months, a U-Boat attack was carried out during the early hours of the 19th. It all started when Fortress HB791/T (F/L Melener) made a radar contact and attacked a surfaced U-Boat some 390 miles ENE of Terceira. The attack was made with eight depth charges, three of which were seen to enter the water with one overshooting and exploding while the other two undershot. The rear gunner was also in a good position to fire a burst of thirty rounds of 0.50-in. The U-Boat was able to escape and nothing further was seen. It was the sixteenth and last attack made a 220's Fortress. In the meantime, the first Liberators had arrived and their first patrol was carried out on the 8th. It was therefore the beginning of the end for the Fortress and another batch left on the 11th for St Eval. At the end of the month, only two Fortress crews remained among eighteen Liberator crews. Only the three Fortress Mk.IIIs were still on charge

The situation remained unchanged in 1945. The three Fortresses soldiered on until the end of April. However, the U-Boat activity was virtually non-existent in the Azores area, so even the Liberator ops were kept at a very low level. As for the Fortresses, only thirteen sorties were flown in four months with the very last being flown on 26 April by HB786/V which was actually a flight back to the UK associated with a reconnaissance mission to Gosport. The Fortress' war with Coastal Command was over.

HB792 - one of the three Fortresses IIIs to have served with Coastal Command. It served with 220 Sqn from June 1944 until March 1945 when it was sent to 3502 SU on the 31st. It would stay at this storage unit until 31 August when it was issued to 251 Sqn where it would fly until December when it was stored at 51 MU. Note that even though it was serving in a Coastal Command unit, this Fortress was left in natural metal finish. The codes 'ZZ' identifying 220 were added in the last stages of the war. The aircraft is seen shortly after its transfer to 251 Sqn and became AD-D. The Fortress is totally unarmed. *(via Robert M. Stitt)*

Confiurmed claims against U-boats - 220 Squadron

Date	Captain	SN	Origin	U-boot	Serial	Code	Nb	Cat.
03.02.43	P/O Kenneth L.H. **Ramsden**	RAF No. 126866	RAF	U-265 (1)	**FL456**	N	1.0	C
07.02.43	F/O George P. **Roberson**	RAF No. 66028	RAF	U-624	**FL459**	J	1.0	C
09.11.43	F/L Roderick P. **Drummond**	AAF No. 91229	RAF	U-707	**FL459**	J	1.0	C
13.03.44	F/O Wilfred R. **Travell**	RAF No. 116983	RAF	U-575 (2)	**FL459**	J	0.16	C
26.09.44	F/L Arthur F. **Wallace**	RAF No. 120620	RAF	U-871 (3)	**FK191**	P	1.0	C

(1): Confirmed after the war, first claimed as damaged.
(2): Shared with a Wellington of 172 Sqn, a 206 Sqn Fortress and USN Grumman Avenger, and three ships.
(3): The pilot was F/O E.C.W. Fieldler.

Total: 4.16

Two hundred and fifty pound depth charges being hoisted into the bomb bay of a Fortress. Fourteen were initially carried by each Fortress, but this load was later halved to allow for extra fuel. The Mk XI depth charge available from the summer of 1942 could be set to explode at an optimum 20ft below the surface.

Summary of the aircraft lost on Operations - 220 Squadron

Date	Crew	S/N	Origin	Serial	Code	Fate
10.08.42	W/O Gordon A. **Sanderson**	RAF No. 742287	RAF	**FK207**	J	†
	F/Sgt Ernest W. **Bristow**	RAF No. 745118	RAF			†
	Sgt David F. **Capel**	Aus. 404602	RAAF			†
	Sgt Victor C. **Fretter**	RAF No. 751381	RAF			†
	Sgt Philip G. **Foster**	RAF No. 1158929	RAF			†
	Sgt Harry **Garcia**	RAF No. 931532	RAF			†
11.08.42	W/C Richard T.F. **Gates**	RAF No. 37064	RAF	**FK204**	N	-
	P/O Kenneth L.H. **Ramsden**	RAF No. 126866	RAF			-
	Sgt Archibald J. **Hill**	RAF No. 1378315	RAF			-
	Sgt Henry **Tasche**	Can./ R.94546	RCAF			-
	Sgt E. **Thornton**	?	?			-
	Sgt J.W. **Wood**	?	?			-
	Sgt William L. **Kean**	RAF No. 1108829	RAF			
	Cpl Robert N. **Morrison**	RAF No. 1192204	RAF			
14.06.43	F/O Charles F. **Callender**	RAF No. 68777	RAF	**FK212**	V	†
	F/O James W. **Verney**	RAF No. 80395	(SA)/RAF			†
	Sgt James W. **Harbidge**	RAF No. 1220213	RAF			†
	F/Sgt Edward **Wright**	RAF No. 978768	RAF			†
	F/Sgt Charles P. **Probst**	RAF No. 979949	RAF			†
	F/Sgt Willaim M. **Comba**	Can./ R.59670	RCAF			†
	Sgt George **Davison**	RAF No. 989245	RAF			†
	F/Sgt Shadrach M. **Frost**	RAF No. 1379682	RAF			†
	Sgt George S. **Patterson**	RAF No. 1051252	RAF			†
25.10.43	S/L Harry A.A. **Webster**	RAF No. 37619	RAF	**FK202**	L	†
	P/O Alfred W. **Dungate**	Can./ J.16441	RCAF			†
	F/O William H. **Offler**	Can./ J.22508	RCAF			†
	F/O James **Walton**	RAF No. 131472	RAF			†
	P/O William T. **Potter**	RAF No. 143930	RAF			†
	Sgt Alexander B. **Christie**	RAF No. 1375581	RAF			†
	Sgt John S. **McKay**	RAF No. 1325202	RAF			†
	W/O2 Maxwell E. **Varney**	Can./ R.17569	RCAF			†
04.12.43	F/O Desmond E. **Morris**	RAF No. 132320	RAF	**FK206**	K	†
	F/Sgt Robert N. **Morrison**	RAF No. 1192204	RAF			†
	F/Sgt James G. **Johnson**	Aus. 408252	RAAF			†
	P/O Harold **Lawson**	RAF No. 149162	RAF			†
	P/O Arthur **Pierce**	Aus. 406868	RAAF			†
	F/Sgt Carl T. **Flack**	Can./ R.121119	RCAF			†
	F/Sgt Joseph E.R. **Boudreault**	Can./ R.125388	RCAF			†
	F/Sgt Michael P. **Campion**	RAF No. 536451	RAF			†
19.12.43	F/O John M. **Ireland**	RAF No. 122500	RAF	**FA697**	T	-
	P/O William G. **Cameron**	Can./ J.21960	RCAF			-
	F/O Charles D. **Collins**	RAF No. 111434	RAF			-
	F/O Ronald K.A. **Grant**	Can./ J.9853	RCAF			-
	F/Sgt Stanley J. **Smith**	RAF No. 978959	RAF			-
	F/Sgt John C.E. **Loftus**	RAF No. 1077388	RAF			-
	Sgt Charles H. **Holyland**	RAF No. 1290781	RAF			-
	Sgt John D. **Newsome**	RAF No. 1074651	RAF			-
	Sgt Henry J. **Coulter**	RAF No. 1605561	RAF			-

Date	Crew	S/N	Origin	Serial	Code	Fate
25.07.44	P/O Eric B. McIlwrick	RAF No. 178743	RAF	FA707	Z	-
	W/O Reginal W. Knight	Can./ R.123432	RCAF			-
	F/O Clarence D. Lamb	Can./ J.23814	RCAF			-
	F/Sgt James Taylor	RAF No. 623968	RAF			-
	F/Sgt Neville V. Ryan	Aus. 422812	RAAF			-
	Sgt Harry G. King	RAF No. 1865325	RAF			-
	Sgt William C. Lyle	RAF No. 1601046	RAF			-
	F/Sgt Harold W. Cousin	Can./ R.170443	RCAF			-
26.07.44	F/L Laurence H. Croft	Can./ J.10615	RCAF	FK189	Y	-
	F/O Garnet H.D. Wilson*	Can./ J.12740	RCAF			-
	F/O Herman Shaak*	Can./ J.21955	RCAF			-
	F/O Thomas P. Owen*	RAF No. 137116	RAF			-
	F/L Reginald G. Philpott*	RAF No. 47532	RAF			-
	W/O R. McLean*	?	RAF			-
	Sgt Philip A. Leegood*	RAF No. 1332073	RAF			-
	Sgt Raymond G. Flower*	RAF No. 575205	RAF			-

*Names not reported. Usual crew of eight as per July-August 1944, but nine people were on board that day.

Total: 8

Summary of the aircraft lost by accident - 220 Squadron

Date	Crew	S/N	Origin	Serial	Code	Fate
30.11.43	F/L George P. Robertson	RAF No. 66028	RAF	FA708	D	-
	Lt Theodore W. Case	O-886098	USAAF			-
	F/O William G. Cameron	Can./J.21960	RCAF			-
19.04.44	Ground accident	-	-	FK198	R	-
02.08.44	F/L Laurence H. Croft (taxi accident, was alone in board)	Can./ J.10615	RCAF	FA706	S	-

Total: 3

WITH OTHER OPERATIONAL SQUADRONS

No. 59 Squadron
Number 59 Squadron was initially a pre-war co-operation unit and its role evolved to strategic reconnaissance when it flew its Blenheims to France at the outbreak of the war. Repatriated to the UK, it added bombing raids and anti-submarine patrols under Coastal Command authority to its repertoire. By 1942, it had relinquished its Hudsons for Liberator Mk.IIIs and the first operation was carried out on 24 October. The squadron was under the leadership of W/C C.C. Bartlett. A few weeks later, the squadron was advised that it would be re-equipped with the Fortress to the great consternation of the personnel. This re-equipment was also accompanied with a change of station, planned to be Chivenor in Devon, north of Plymouth (the squadron was located at Thorney Island, near Portsmouth, at the time), so it could participate in the coverage of the U-boat transit routes. There was actually a good reason for the switch to the Fortress. The RAF was short of Liberators and did not have enough in reserve for the existing squadrons, especially those using the long range Liberators. At the same time, the RAF now had enough Fortresses to allow the conversion of a third squadron. The last sortie on Liberators was carried out on 10 December and three days later conversion training began with Fortress FK202. Other Fortresses arrived at the squadron (FK188 and FL450 on the 15th; FK209, FL462, FL463 and FL464 on the 31st; and FK198 and FK189 arrived on 9 and 11 January respectively. Conversion training was also carried out on a Fortress Mk.I (AN519) and the rest of December was spent focusing on the conversion which was marred by the accident of FK188 on the 30th when it was struck by Hampden AE370 of 415 Squadron after the latter swung off the runway while taxiing. The Fortress needed six months of intensive repairs, but would return to service.

The training was completed by mid-January and the move to Chivenor began on 21 January with the first patrol undertaken two days later, F/O Alexander R. Neilson (RCAF) taking off at 04.52 in FK205/B and returning ten hours later with nothing to report. The next day, F/O Howard A.L. Moran (RAAF) took off in the same aircraft and soon reached his patrol area flying at 2500 feet. At 13.10, a Ju88 was sighted off the starboard beam some 800 yards away and flying on a parallel course. Both aircraft immediately climbed for the cloud base some 500 feet above while the Ju88 prepared to attack. The Ju88 fired at the Fortress, but scored no hits, while in return the rear gunner of the Fortress was able to fire a 5-6 second burst, for a total of 160 rounds, as the Junkers passed under the Fortress and entered cloud. Moran then took evasive action and the Ju88 was not seen again. The rest of the patrol was uneventful and the Fortress landed back at base six and a half hours later with its fourteen depth charges still on board. Four more patrols were performed before the end of the month, and 31 more in February, most being uneventful. However, that month, on the 6th, P/O Stephen G.

After having been used by the RAE for LRASV trials since July 1942, FK202 was then issued to 59 Sqn and coded 'B'. When 59 was re-equipped, FK202 was passed on to 220 as 'L'. It was lost during a patrol off the Azores on 25.10.43. *(Andrew Thomas)*

DuPlooy attacked a U-Boat while piloting FA463/D. Airborne at 09.33, the Fortress flew the outbound track until it reached its PLE (Prudent Limit of Endurance) without incident and turned for home. At 16.20 a U-boat was sighted four miles away on the starboard side. The Fortress approached and at two miles, it was seen to be fully surfaced and travelling at an estimated speed of six knots. DuPlooy turned to the right for an up-sun attack while attempting to lose height rapidly, but as he was too close to the target when it was sighted, he could not descend fast enough to make the run. At 1000 yards, the upper gunner opened fire and numerous hits were noticed on the U-boat's conning tower. When the Fortress was at 800 yards, the Germans returned fire with their cannon, but they failed to inflict any damage. As the Fortress passed overhead, it was the turn of the rear gunner to open fire and hits were again scored on the tower. DuPlooy turned the aircraft to the right and this time it was the turn of the beam gunner to open fire as the U-boat was diving. Completing a 200-degree turn, the Fortress dropped five depth charges from fifty feet across the U-boat's track from port to starboard. The charges exploded, but no further results were observed. Otherwise, at the end of the month, the squadron began to receive the first Fortress IIs to enter Coastal Command service with FA703 arriving. FA698 and FA704 would follow in March.

In March 1943, the squadron sent its Fortresses out on 54 patrols. The month started with another attack, again by FL463/D, but this time captained by F/O Neville Barson. The Fortress had been airborne for five hours when the beam gunner sighted a surfaced U-boat one or two miles away on the starboard side. Barson prepared to attack at once, reversing his course and reducing power to lose height rapidly to make an up-sun attack. As the Fortress approached, the U-boat (U-223) opened fire for a few seconds and, unlike the previous attack on 6 February, the Fortress was hit and sustained considerable damage to the hydraulic system among other things. Despite this, Barson continued his attack and dropped five depth charges which were seen to explode, the nearest at six metres from the U-boat. When passing over the U-boat, the rear gunner opened fire, but no casualties were seen among the sailors present on the deck. Soon after, the U-boat dived while the Fortress tried, unsuccessfully, for the next quarter of an hour to locate it again. Barson eventually turned the aircraft for home where it landed at 18.37 after ten and a half hours in the air. On 3 March a third attack was made by F/O Henry D. Kelvin while flying FL462/C. Five depth charges were dropped, but no significant results were reported. As stated before, patrolling was not without danger as the Luftwaffe was very active over this part of the ocean. On 23 March, FK209/J took off at 04.30 for a patrol over the Bay of Biscay. The Fortress was flown by F/O Richard J. Weatherhead (RCAF). The flight seems to have been uneventful until the radio operator was heard stating they were being attacked by an enemy aircraft. Nothing more was heard of the eight crewmembers and the Fortress was indeed claimed by *Oberleutant* Hermann Hortsmann of 13./KG 40. The squadron was also badly hit three days later when FA698/V crashed into a hillside in low cloud while preparing to land at Chivenor on return from a patrol. Three crewmembers were killed in this accident. Sadly, they died the day before the squadron ceased operations on the Fortress. Indeed, on the 27th, F/O M. Charlton (RAAF) in FA704/R and P/O S. DuPlooy in FL463/D were sent out on patrol, the former returning after eleven hours and 15 minutes of flight and the latter after ten hours and 20 minutes. The same day, the squadron began its move back to Thorney Island to be re-equipped with the Liberator once more, but the Mk.V this time. In all, the squadron flew 91 sorties on Fortresses representing 965 operational hours during which three U-boat attacks were made and two aircraft lost.

Summary of the aircraft lost on Operations - 59 Squadron

Date	Crew	S/N	Origin	Serial	Code	Fate
23.03.43	F/O Richard J. **Weatherhead**	Can./ J.6992	RCAF	**FK209**	J	†
	F/O William C. **Zapfe**	Can./ J.7024	RCAF			†
	Sgt William J. **Arnold**	Can./ R.106166	RCAF			†
	P/O George **Cojocar**	Can./ J.16374	RCAF			†
	Sgt Frank **Spino**	Can./ R.75875	RCAF			†
	Sgt Clarence L. **Copping**	Can./ R.77233	RCAF			†
	Sgt Richard G. **Montgomery**	Can./ R.106426	RCAF			†
	P/O Robert A. **Philipps**	RAF No. 128609	RAF			†
26.03.43	F/L James L. **Heron**	RAF No. 43285	RAF	**FA698**	V	-
	P/O Donald H. **McLean**	Can./ J.16692	RCAF			-
	Sgt Arden **Kenney**	RAF No. 1370313	RAF			-
	F/Sgt Robert S. **Sanderlin**	Can./ R.82680	RCAF			†
	Sgt James F. **Clark**	RAF No. 1128327	RAF			-
	Sgt Jeffrey **Fage**	RAF No. 1172715	RAF			†
	P/O Denis M. **Dunn**	RAF No. 141755	RAF			†

Total: 2

No. 206 Squadron

Flying the Lockheed Hudson from 1940, 206 was selected to become the second squadron to operate the Fortress. It had moved to Benbecula, in the Outer Hebrides, off the west coast of Scotland, in early July and had had a new CO since the end of June. Wing Commander J.R.S. Romanes had earned the DFC in July 1940 during an earlier tour with 206. Things became concrete on 20 July when the first pilots were detached to 220 Squadron for four-engine conversion. Ten days later, the first two Fortresses, FL453 and FL457, arrived at the squadron. On 4 August, more Fortresses were collected directly from Burtonwood (FL454, FK208 and FK213), followed by FL460, FK210 and FL452 on the 12th and FK184 and FL455 four days later. In August, operational duties with the Hudsons were reduced, while training was carried out at the same time, and ended on the 27th with the last patrol on type. Between 1 and 18 September, the squadron focused on the conversion, based mainly on navigation exercises, and on 19 September, F/L William Roxburgh performed the first Fortress patrol which took place between 07.41 and 16.11. It was rather uneventful except for the sighting of an empty raft. This patrol was followed by five more before the end of the month. The squadron resumed full anti-submarine work from 1 October. That month 59 sorties were carried out for more than 520 hours of patrol. Also, changes occurred regarding armament. The initial load of twelve depth charges and two 250-lb anti-submarine bombs was progressively changed to fourteen depth charges, as the 250-lb bombs endangered the aircraft when dropped too low, then to only seven depth charges from the end of October 1942 onwards. The remaining space in the bomb bay was filled with a jettisonnable fuel tank of 1550 l (341 Imp G). The first U-boats were sighted on 5 October by Fortress 'B', captained by F/O A.E. Bland, and an attack was made on the second, but no results were observed. The next day a tragedy occurred when Fortress FL454/J crashed into the sea immediately after take-off. Five of the crew were killed. The next U-boat attack took place on the 21st. Again, no results were observed (Fortress FK208/B). Two more attacks would be undertaken on surfaced U-boats before the end of the month. On the 27th, Fortress FL457/F (P/O R.L. Cowey) had taken off at 06.30 to fly cover for a convoy. Five hours later the crew spotted a U-boat travelling at conning tower depth. The U-boat was attacked and all seven charges were dropped 25 feet ahead of the swirl as the U-boat dived. The results observed were a patch of oil 100 yards long, but little other evidence of a kill. In fact, it was a kill as U-627 was lost with its entire crew of 44. It was the first patrol for U-627, but also the first U-boat destroyed by a Fortress and the second U-boat sinking by a long-range land-based aircraft. The second attack occurred on the last day of the month (FL457/F again, W/O R.S. Weir), but no results were observed. In November, 67 sorties were flown for 676 hours on patrol. Despite this increased figure compared to October, only one U-boat sighting and attack was made. This was probably due to the fact that a part of the U-boat fleet had sailed to the western Mediterranean following the Allied landings in North Africa. The only attack took place on the 25th

No. 206 Sqn's commanding Officer W/C James Romanes (left) with his crew at Benbecula in late 1942. From left to right: W/O Alan Marriott to his left, W/O R. Stares, Sgt J.H. Norris, F/Sgt S. Bickell on the wing, F/Sgt D.L. Baldwin, Sgt W.H.S. Clough and W/O G.W. Cairns. On the wing, Sgt J.H. Norris, and F/Sgt S. Bickell. *(206 Sqn via Robert M. Stitt)*

when F/O W. Roxburgh (FK213/C) dropped his seven depth charges which exploded 120 yards ahead of the swirl 28 seconds after the U-boat disappeared. Light coloured oil was seen two minutes later. The next U-boat attack occurred on 11 December (FL460/H, F/O John Owen). The sighting was made after close to seven hours on patrol covering a convoy. The U-boat was seen making six knots on a course of 250 degrees, slightly on the port bow and one and half miles away. The conning tower, the forward catwalk and net cutter could be clearly distinguished. Flying Officer Owen delivered his attack on the port quarter of the U-boat at twenty degrees to its track while the tip of the periscope and the stern were still visible. The crew could see the explosions of the six depth charges dropped touching the port side of the swirl. The U-boat seems to have been damaged as a photograph showed a surfacing U-boat with a large jagged hole torn through the forward end of the apron of its conning tower. Half an hour later, a second U-boat was seen by the crew and attacked with the remaining depth charge from thirty feet which exploded in the front portion of the swirl. The tail gunner stated that a great volume of water was thrown up by the explosion and was greater than the previous attack. For this reason, the U-boat was claimed as damaged too. Two hours later, another U-boat was found, but, having no more depth charges on board, only a mock attack could be made. If this crew seems to have been lucky, then their run of good fortune came to an end three days later when they failed to return from another patrol (FL453/A). Despite many efforts made to locate possible survivors, the ASR missions were not successful. The rest of December was uneventful and during the month, despite the bad weather prevailing over the area, 53 sorties were flown for 450 hours on patrol.

On 15 January 1943, after two weeks of uneventful patrols, the squadron filed its second success against the U-boats. Fortress FL452/G, with P/O Leslie Clark in command, was tasked with conducting anti-submarine sweeps around a convoy. A surfaced submarine was sighted six miles away and Clark attacked with all seven depth charges. Even though three failed to release, the U-boat was seen to slip backwards below the surface at a steep angle in what appeared to the crew to be an uncontrolled dive. The U-boat, U-632, though damaged, was not sunk, and would survive another few months before it was finally sunk, by a Liberator of 86 Squadron, on 6 April. It was claimed 'probably seriously damaged even sunk' by the 206 crew on return. This attack would be the only one recorded in January over 59 sorties totalling 520 flying hours. The efforts continued with the same intensity in February, and on the 9th, Fortress FK195/L (S/L Richard Patrick) was tasked with escorting a destroyer towing a corvette. A U-boat was sighted after two hours and attacked. A stick of six depth charges straddled U-614 forward of its conning tower, causing the U-boat to lift out of the water and appear to sink. Actually, U-614 was later able to regain St-Nazaire. The rest of the month was uneventful. In March, no less than five attacks on U-boats were made. On the 2nd, F/L L.M. Nelson, captain of FK195/L, after having sighted a

Fortress FL451 seen shortly after it had been taken on charge by 206 Sqn early in August 1942. The squadron's code 'VX', still in force during the summer 1942, would soon be discontinued. It is not known whether the codes 'VX-D' are red or black. (*Robert M. Stitt*)

View of FK190/J of No. 206 Sqn at Benbecula. It was mainly used for training and transportation flights, only a handful of operational are recorded while flying with 206 Sqn.

periscope and a feather one and a half miles off the port bow, dived to attack, but within thirty seconds the U-boat had dived and vanished. No attack was carried out as the sun was blinding the crew. This was followed by another attack on 11 March while on a convoy escort (F/Sgt F.S. Willis in FK208/B) and even though four depth charges were dropped, the U-boat was able to escape unscathed. Better results were observed, however, by P/O Leslie G. Clark (FK208/B) after his crew spotted a U-boat hiding in a rain squall behind a convoy. An excellent straddle produced a heavy oil patch that would later prove to mark the end of U-384. For this action, Clark was awarded the DFC a couple of weeks later. On 25 March, FK195/L, with F/L William Roxburgh in command, attacked another U-boat. After five and a half hours on patrol, while flying at 3500 feet, a U-boat was sighted ten degrees on the starboard bow, about four or five miles distant, fully surfaced, and steering a course of 240 degrees at an estimated speed of 5-6 knots. An immediate attack was delivered and the aircraft released six depth charges from about 200 feet in a dive. The U-boat was straddled, three on one side and three the other. In view of the nature of the attack, a dive, the spacing was considerably less than 100 feet. The U-boat was still surfaced after the explosion and may have been listing to port, probably partly submerging before the stern re-appeared after a few seconds in a sort of rolling motion and at a very steep angle (estimated at over 45 degrees). It hung in this position, as the Fortress ran in to attack with its remaining depth charges from fifty feet, sinking straight down just as the second attack was being made along its length from stern to bow. A disturbance in the water in the estimated position of the bow followed and after ten minutes the accumulated oil measured about 1000 yards by 600 yards with floating yellow and white debris. This is how U-469 ended its cruise which had lasted less than nine days. Finally, two days later, FK195/L, this time captained by F/O A.C.I. Samuel, sealed the fate of U-169. Attacked from 2,000 feet, the U-boat first returned fire without accuracy before receiving the first cluster of depth charges. The submarine was seen to roll over and then reappear with its bow up at a sharp angle. A second attack was seen to fall in a white foam patch. As the Fortress drew away from this attack the bows were seen to assume a more acute angle and the rear gunner was able to fire at the keel of the U-boat. Men were scrambling about on the conning tower as she sank in 20-30 seconds. Without a doubt, March had been a very successful month with three U-boats sunk in 62 sorties and more than 600 hours on patrol.

April was also very intense with three attacks reported. On 7 April, Fortress FK213/C, piloted by P/O L.G. Clark, was flying at 250 feet when a U-boat was sighted on a track 270°. The captain turned to starboard and dived to the attack subsequently lengthening the approach by a turn to port to ensure enough time to open the bomb doors. However, when in the attacking position and with the release button pressed, the bomb doors were not fully open and the depth charges automatically hung up. The aircraft flew over

Nice photo of FA702/P during a patrol. This Fortress arrived in the UK in November 1942, but its first operational assignment with 206 was in April 1943. The victim of an accident in August 1943, it was repaired and stored from September to April 1944 when it was issued to 1674 HCU. It was withdrawn from use in September 1945 and sold to International Alloys in 1947. *(Robert M. Stitt)*

the lucky surfaced U-boat and the rear gunner fired fifty rounds at the conning tower with some success. The Fortress made a complete turn to port and the crew observed the submarine submerging rapidly. Then the port beam gunner opened fire, about 100 rounds, and reported some more hits on the conning tower. Clark approached again, but this time the U-boat had totally disappeared. The Fortress circled for five minutes before, as nothing else happened, Clark decided to resume the patrol. On the 22nd, FL451/D (F/O W.S. Weir) conducted another attack, dropping six depth charges after the conning tower had disappeared. No significant results were observed. The next attack, which was carried out on the 24th, was more successful. The attack was conducted by F/O Cowey (responsible for the first kill the previous December) flying FL451/D. A submarine was spotted some ten miles ahead of the convoy as the Fortress swept its path. Cowey attacked at right angles to the U-boat's track. The first six depth charges lifted the vessel almost clear of the surface. A second attack was made before some 25 survivors were seen swimming amid small pieces of floating wreckage. The cruise of U-710, which had started on 15 April from Kiel, ended and Cowey would receive the DFC for repeated successful actions since the previous autumn. May was much calmer with 400 hours on patrol and only one unsuccessful attack reported (FK210/, S/L R.C. Patrick). On the administrative side, W/C J.R.S. Romanes relinquished command to W/C R.B. Thomson on the 16th. Thomson, a pre-war Auxiliary officer with No. 612 Squadron, had just been awarded the DSO for flying Wellingtons with No. 172 Squadron.

Fortunes changed in June, however, but it was now the turn of 206 to sustain losses. The first warning came on the 5th, when Fortress FA703/A (F/O A.T. Lovell) was attacked by nine Ju88s, but escaped undamaged. One week later, Fortress FA704/R, piloted by W/C Ronald B. Thomson, spotted a U-boat on the surface and dived at once to attack. The U-boat made no attempt to dive and when the Fortress was fifty feet above the surface and about 300-400 yards from the submarine, the U-boat opened fire with its flak guns. As the Fortress passed over the submarine, the depth charges were dropped as the aircraft was hit along the fuselage. The U-boat's bow rose out of the water until the hull was vertical before it slid backwards into the sea. In its last moments, the gunners of U-417 were accurate as the Fortress' starboard inner engine began to pour a lot of smoke. The CO tried to feather the airscrew, but before it was done, the two port engines started to give trouble with smoke pouring from the wing. In such conditions a safe return was impossible and Thomson had no choice but to ditch the aircraft. The Fortress sank in ninety seconds, but all crewmembers were able to get into a single dinghy and after many attempts to rescue the crew were delayed by heavy seas (at the cost of a USN PBY Catalina and the lives of eight crewmen), they were rescued three days later with all but one in very good shape. For this action, the CO, Flight Lieutenant J.F. Clark and Flying Officer J.L. Humphries receieced the DFC. By that time, the presence of U-boats in the North Atlantic was almost non-existent so the squadron (along with 220 Squadron) was detached to the southwest

Fortress FA704 seen on patrol in 1943. It served with 59 Sqn as 'R' before being handed over to the 206. It continued to fly as 'R' and was eventually shot down by U-417 on 11.06.43. The crew survived. *(Robert M. Stitt)*

of England to better cover the U-boat transit routes in the southern Bay of Biscay. On 17 June, F/O Leslie Clark (FL457/F) damaged a U-boat. As with the attack conducted a week earlier by W/C Thomson, the crew of the U-boat elected to engage the Fortress rather than dive. That was a new tactic the Coastal Command crews had to deal with from now on. In this case, the Fortress was not hit in the two attacks Clark made and eleven depth charges were dropped (the Fortress now carried them under the wings as well). Until the end of August, the squadron continued to fly patrols from the United Kingdom, about 100 sorties representing 700 hours being flown, but with the North Atlantic convoy routes secure, it (along with 220) was temporarily stood down and Liberator units took over the role in the area.

However, a new role was waiting for the Fortress crews. The zone between the Azores and the Bay of Biscay, and from the Azores to beyond the Canary Islands to the west coast of Africa, where the U-boats were still a real threat, needed reinforcements. After months of negotiations, Portugal and the Allies reached an agreement and the RAF was allowed to operate from the Azores at Lagens. The Fortress in this case was a better choice than the Liberator as it had shorter take-off and landing performance, so was better suited to the operating conditions at Lagens. Preparations and the move took place in September and into the first fortnight of October because some modifications had to be carried out. A '1' was painted on the squadron's aircraft to differentiate them from those of 220 Squadron (which had a '2' applied). An extra fuel tank of 1550 litres was also installed in the bomb bay to extend endurance to fifteen hours. The first Fortress, FA710/M flown by the CO, eventually landed at Lagens on 18 October. The balance of the fifteen aircraft arrived over the following days and the last landed on the 25th. In the meantime, patrols resumed, with the first A/S sweep carried out on the 21st by F/O R.G. Rigg (RCAF) and crew in FA710/M. In all, sixteen patrols were flown before the end of the month, for 100 hours on patrol, but no U-boats were sighted. More than 800 hours of patrols were flown in November, close to eighty sorties, but no U-boat attack was made as none were sighted. It was a bit frustrating for the squadron, as 220 was luckier with seven U-boat attacks made that month and one submarine sunk. The run of bad luck was reinforced by the fact that one Fortress had come close to being shot down by the ships it was escorting on the 19th (FL452/F, F/L W.L. Vickerestaff) when the aircraft broke cloud over the convoy. Even though the ships were notified, the AA still opened fire and forced the captain to take evasive action. The AA finally ceased, but holed the Fortress in various locations in the fuselage without injuring anyone on board. To make things worse, the squadron lost a Fortress on the 30th when FK208/B crashed at Gibraltar with no survivors. The Fortress had been tasked to escort convoy SL140 when, two and a half hours after departing Lagens on the 29th, the crew was instructed by base

Fortress FK190 '1-J' while flying a patrol off Lagens in the Azores. Note the aerial, located on top of the rear fuselage, that is part of the search transmit component of ASV Mk II radar, equipment inherited from the RAE where the aircraft was used for trials. It wasn't removed for some reason. Issued to 206 in March 1943, it would carry out few operational patrols and was mainly used for training purposes before becoming the victim of an accident in August 1943. It returned to the squadron in November 1943 only to be passed to 220 in April. It is presumed that the aerial was removed during this second period of use. *(Robert M. Stitt)*

to land at Gibraltar on completion of the sortie. In the early hours of the 30th, the Fortress was approaching Gibraltar as it was announced that the airfield was closing down due to fog. As the Fortress did not have enough fuel to reach Port Lyautey in Morocco, the captain, F/S Denis J.A. Mitchell had no choice but to ditch or try to land at Gibraltar. Whatever he chose to do, his attempt failed and FK208/B crashed ten miles south of the Rock. December would also be frustratingly free of any action despite seventy sorties and 730 hours on patrol.

The new year began with a new blow for 206. On 6 January 1944, Fortress FA705/U and its crew were posted missing. The Fortress was actually shot down by the flak guns of U-270 during its third strafing run. The Fortress was hit in the starboard inner engine which caught fire. It was seen to lose height, but despite this, S/L J. Pinhorn, the captain, was able to release his four depth charges some 100 to 300 yards from the U-boat. The aircraft then dived into the ocean 300 metres from the U-Boat engulfed in flames. All nine crewmen lost their lives including an extra passenger, S/L Ralph Brown, the squadron's navigation officer. The flak had become a major threat now as the U-Boat crews, when caught on surface, chose to fight it out and the flak was an effective weapon against a low and massive silhouette like a Fortress. A few days later, on the 14th, F/L G.J.M. Hart, in FA700/R, was engaged by flak while attacking a U-Boat (four depth charges were dropped at fifty feet). While only hit a few times, it forced the Fortress to remain at a distance hoping the captain of the U-Boat would dive, the only time now when a U-Boat was really vulnerable. The U-Boat stayed on the surface for the next two hours and nothing happened before the Fortress was obliged to set course for base. These would be the only attacks of the month in over 630 hours on patrol. However that month was also the beginning of the end of the Fortress' presence in the Azores. The USN began to send construction units to build new facilities with the aim of operating USN PB2Y Liberator squadrons under British control. February was uneventful, but in March one U-Boat attack was reported on the 13th by FA700/R captained by F/L A.D. Beaty. Caught on the surface, the U-boat forced Beaty to abort his attack and take evasive action due to the volume of flak. The Fortress initiated a second attack from a 90° angle to starboard of the U-Boat and even though the flak opened fire once more, Beaty managed to drop four depth charges, one falling to port, three to starboard. The flak ceased when they exploded and the U-boat was seen to sink with its hull as a high angle. Long patches of oil were also sighted. The Fortress remained in the area, but could not stay much longer and the U-Boat (U-575) was later finished off by a Fortress of 220 Squadron (FL459/J). The sinking of U-575 would also be shared with a Wellington of No. 172 Squadron, a USN carrier-borne Avenger, a Canadian frigate and two American destroyers.

Three days later, the squadron sent its last two Fortresses, FK186/X (F/O R.C. Hales) and FK198/W (F/O F.W. Rigg – RCAF) on patrol while preparations for the return to the UK were already underway. In all, the squadron had flown more than 3000 hours of patrols from the Azores. It was earmarked to re-equip with the Liberator in the UK, so some 65 personnel and five Fortresses (FK186, FK198, FK213 and FL460) were left with 220 Squadron. The remaining Fortresses made their journey back to England from 19 March onwards before they were stored pending overhaul and new assignment. In all, the squadron was credited with flying the Fortresses on 8400 hours of patrols over 864 sorties and achieving 23 attacks on U-boats leading to the destruction of nine of them, one being shared.

Confiurmed claims against U-boats - 206 Squadron

Date	Captain	SN	Origin	U-boot	Serial	Code	Nb	Cat.
27.10.42	P/O Robert L. **Cowey**	RAF No. 126097	RAF	U-627	**FL457**	F	1.0	C
15.01.43	P/O Leslie G. **Clark**	RAF No. 131639	RAF	U-632 *	**FL452**	G	1.0	P
11.03.43	P/O Leslie G. **Clark**	RAF No. 131639	RAF	U-384	**FK208**	B	1.0	C
25.03.43	F/L William **Roxburgh**	RAF No. 63802	RAF	U-469	**FK195**	L	1.0	C
27.03.43	F/O Adrian C.I. **Samuel**	RAF No. 100072	RAF	U-169	**FK195**	L	1.0	C
24.04.43	F/O Robert L. **Cowey**	RAF No. 126097	RAF	U-710	**FL451**	D	1.0	C
11.06.43	W/C Ronald B. **Thomson**	AAF No. 90370	RAF	U-417	**FA704**	R	1.0	C
13.03.44	F/L Arthur D. **Beaty**	RAF No. 60550	RAF	U-575**	**FA700**	R	0.16	C

*Claimed as probably sunk. Damaged only, sunk the following April.
**: Shared with a Wellington of 172 Sqn, a 220 Sqn Fortress and USN Grumman Avenger, and three ships.

Total: 7.16

Summary of the aircraft lost on Operations - 206 Squadron

Date	Crew	S/N	Origin	Serial	Code	Fate
06.10.42	P/O Jack E. Delarue	Aus. 402322	RAAF	FL454	J	†
	Sgt Frederick A. Robinson	RAF No. 1376615	RAF			†
	Sgt James C.H.R. Jaeger	RAF No. 1382407	RAF			†
	Sgt David S. Coutts	RAF No. 1023023	RAF			-
	Sgt James Hunt	?	RAF			-
	Sgt John F. Guppy	Aus. 406452	RAAF			†
	Sgt John B. Taplin	Aus. 407607	RAAF			†
14.12.42	F/O John Owen	RAF No. 63800	RAF	FL453	A	†
	Sgt Robert N. Hildred	RAF No. 1333535	RAF			†
	Sgt Rupert Bentley	RAF No. 1115124	RAF			†
	F/Sgt Eric Crowe	RAF No. 964953	RAF			†
	Sgt William J. Parnell	RAF No. 1163993	RAF			†
	Sgt Garfield C. Wilson	NZ411113	RNZAF			†
	Sgt Walter Shanks	RAF No. 1067932	RAF			†
11.06.43	W/C Ronald B. Thomson	AAF No. 90370	RAF	FA704	R	-
	F/Sgt Anthony F. Chisnall	RAF No. 778626	RAF			-
	F/L John F. Clark	RAF No. 106550	RAF			-
	F/O John L. Humphreys	RAF No. 133343	RAF			-
	Sgt Frank Sweetlove	RAF No. 1269197	RAF			-
	Sgt Ronald A. Senior	RAF No. 1115843	RAF			-
	Sgt R. Owens	?	RAF			-
	F/L Arthur R.D. Barratt *	RAF No. 40354	RAF			-
29.11.43	F/Sgt Denis J.A. Mitchener	RAF No. 1450109	RAF	FK208	B	†
	F/Sgt John Wilson	RAF No. 1120348	RAF			†
	F/Sgt Donald B. Brown	RAF No. 1066461	RAF			†
	W/O David S. Coutts	RAF No. 1023023	RAF			†
	F/Sgt James Stone	RAF No. 751932	RAF			†
	F/O Arthur E. Moule	RAF No. 126145	RAF			†
	Sgt Robert A.C. Burnett	RAF No. 1270447	RAF			†
	Sgt Ronald A. Senior	RAF No. 1115843	RAF			†
06.01.44	S/L Anthony J. Pinhorn	RAF No. 42468	(CAN)/RAF	FA705	U	†
	F/L Ralph Brown	RAF No. 78250	RAF			†
	F/Sgt Thomas Eckersley	RAF No. 1533557	RAF			†
	F/O Francis D. Roberts	RAF No. 122972	RAF			†
	F/O Joseph H. Duncan	RAF No. 126994	RAF			†
	W/O Ronald N. Stares	RAF No. 931486	RAF			†
	W/O Oliver A. Keddy	Can./ R.88434	RCAF			†
	W/O Donald L. Heard	Can./ R.105458	RCAF			†
	Sgt Robert Fabian	RAF No. 1288265	RAF			†

Total: 5

*Station Armament Officer

WITH THE BOMBER COMMAND

No. 214 Squadron (code BU):
The return of the Boeing Fortress to Bomber Command is directly connected with the formation of No. 100 (SD) Group in November 1943. This Group was formed to consolidate the increasingly complex business of electronic warfare and countermeasures within one organisation. The group was responsible for the development, operational trial and use of electronic warfare and countermeasures equipment. It was initially formed with Mosquitoes, to harass the German night fighter forces, and bomber squadrons utilising various specialist electronic jamming devices to disrupt enemy radio communications and radar. Number 214 Squadron was one of those bomber squadrons and the first to be equipped with Fortresses, the other types used being Halifaxes and Liberators (and the Short Stirling, but only for a short time). Initially a standard night bomber squadron flying Stirlings, 214 was chosen to operate the Boeing Fortress. It was withdrawn from the frontline to convert to the new type and role in January 1944. The squadron was based at Sculthorpe, north of Norwich, and had been commanded by W/C D.J. McGlinn since July 1943. The squadron took charge of its first Fortress (SR386) on 28 January; followed by SR377 and SR383 on 29 January; SR376, SR378, SR380, SR381, SR382, SR384, SR385, SR387 and SR388 on 2 February; SR379 on the 3rd; and, finally, SR389 on the 5th. Training started quickly and the first night exercise was performed on the 5th. By 20 April, the squadron was ready to be sent on operations and that night four Fortresses were dispatched for bomber support - S/L W.S. Day (RCAF) in SR388/H and F/O R.J. Waters (RCAF) in SR386/N in support of a raid to La Chapelle (269 bombers), and P/O G.A. Mackie in SR377/M and F/L C.C. Puterbough (RCAF) in SR382/B to Ottignies (196 bombers). From now on, 214 would send an average of four Fortresses in support of Bomber Command raids. Five more operations were carried out before the end of the month. Compared to the bombers, the length of a typical support sortie was shorter and between 4.5 to 5 hours, and sometimes much less than this. In May, fifty sorties were carried out, and the first incidents occurred. On the 6th, F/O C.E. Lye (RNZAF) in SR381/F, while flying support for 149 bombers, was chased by a Bf109 for six minutes, but the gunners were able to fire at it and claim it as damaged. Five nights later, SR382/B (P/O J.D. Cassan) encountered a Ju88, but the starboard and port waist gunners both opened fire and that discouraged the night fighter which broke away. These encounters could be taken as a warning as, eventually, the first Fortress (SR384/A) failed to return from a bomber support sortie on the 24th. It had taken off at 23.40, with P/O A.J.N. Hockley (RAAF) in command, for Antwerp as 51 bombers had been detailed to attack the city. It was caught by a night fighter (Oblt Herman Leube of 4./NJG 3) and shot down. Of the nine crewmembers, Hockley and one other were killed. The rest of the crew was taken prisoner. In the meantime, the squadron had moved to Oulton on the 16th, still in the Norwich area and a bit further east than Sculthorpe.

The squadron had its revenge a few nights later when SR386/N (Wing Commander D.J. McGlinn) went into combat with a Me410 (more probably a Bf110) during which the gunners were able to score hits and it was claimed as destroyed on return. The Germans held their own as the Fortress returned damaged, but with all on board safe. This operation was part of the support for the D-Day landings

Despite being painted black, this Fortress from 214 Sqn SR376, coded BU-C, seems not to have its ECM equipment installed yet. Of the first batch of Fortresses from the 8th AF assigned to the squadron, three were used to train crews (SR376, SR385 and SR387). The landscape behind and the absence of the individual letter painted on the tail, let think that this photo was taken at the end of the winter 1943-1944. *(via Andrew Thomas)*

A fully operational Fortress Mk.III (KH999/BU-W) with all of its electronic equipment including the prominent Jostle transmission mast behind the radio boom, the nose radome containing the H2S scanner and the rear mounted Airborne Grocer and Dina aerial.

to come in the next hours. Of the five Fortresses flying that night, two had to return early, SR382/B (S/L J.R. Jeffery) with the port outer engine on fire, and SR377/M (F/O C.E. Lye – RNZAF) following an oxygen system failure and a weak starboard inner that was giving some trouble. The near war-weary Fortress Mk.IIs handed over by the 8th AF were causing trouble after such a long time in use. One week later, it was the turn of SR377/M (F/O T.J. Bayliss) to be intercepted by a Ju88, but it was kept at bay by the gunners and the Junkers gave up before it was hit. In the last minutes of 21 June, three Fortresses took off for another bomber support op (Gelsenkirchen). Only one would return unscathed (SR388/H). The two others, SR381/F and SR382/B, were caught by night fighters. The latter crashed in the Netherlands. Five of the crew were killed, three became PoWs, and only one crewmember, W/O D.R. Jennings (RCAF) managed to evade capture. Fortress SR381/F was luckier, having been hit in the right inner engine after an attack by a Bf110, and attacked a second time by a Ju88 that caused further damage, but was damaged in return. The Fortress was able to continue to England and managed to perform an emergency landing at Woodbridge where it unfortunately collided with a Lancaster from 61 Squadron and was eventually written off. During the attack, F/S Alfred Stanley, the wireless operator/air gunner, was wounded at the head, shoulder and arms and in spite of his injuries spent a lot of energy to repair the intercom damaged in the combat. He then continued to work to obtain fixes to assist the navigator and to bring the aircraft home. For his actions he was awarded the DFM. Partially because of these losses, 214 was stood down for two weeks. In the meantime, the squadron took charge of the first Fortress Mk.IIIs, HB763 and HB774, which arrived on the 7th.

In July, the squadron participated in sixteen raids totaling 118 sorties. Progressively, the number of aircraft engaged increased with, for example, eleven aircraft detailed on the 23rd and the 24th and twelve on the 28th. In August, the rhythm was maintained with close to 100 sorties over fifteen raids. However, one Fortress failed to return (HB763/T). It was downed over Belgium with the loss four crewmembers and the remaining six taken prisoner. The Fortress was supporting the raid on Russelheim by 412 Lancasters of Nos. 1, 3 and 6 Groups. Another Fortress (HB767/A) was lost two weeks later while participating in a raid to Frankfurt (387 bombers). It ditched in the Channel with only one survivor. After having participated in 21 raids during September, only twelve were flown in October. The danger was constant and night fighters were regularly seen, but few combats reported. Shortly after midnight on the 7th, F/O G.L. Wright (HB774/G) landed at base after 5.5 hours of flight and reported that his Fortress had been attacked first by a Ju88, then by a Fw190. Both German aircraft were claimed as damaged. Another Fortress was also attacked by an unidentified enemy aircraft that night (HB793/B – S/L E.V. Miller, RCAF) and also claimed a damaged after one of the air gunners scored some hits. The German fighters were very active in October and would be responsible for the loss of HB800 at the end of the month. The Fortress was intercepted by a Fw190. The fighter attacked with reddish tracers from below on the right beam. Immediately after, the same thing occurred on the left beam. The 190 was seen going over the top and round to the left beam. One of the crew called for a corkscrew when he saw that the enemy aircraft was going to attack from the left quarter. Strikes were seen on the engine of the fighter which turned away and was never seen again. However, the Fortress had been badly hit and the pilot, F/Sgt J.P. Robertson (RNZAF), made a perfect belly-landing on three engines at Ford. No one on board was injured. The Fortress was first considered as being able to return to service quickly, and the repair job was given to Scottish Aviation, but it soon became clear that major repairs had to be undertaken and the Fortress was re-categorised B on 11 December. HB800 arrived at Scottish Aviation works on 10 January 1945, but after a long investigation, it was decided that it was not economical to undertake any repairs. The end of the war being so close and the fact RAF had enough Fortresses on hand was probably taken into account in arriving at this decision. Therefore, HB800 was struck off charge on 12 February 1945 as a total write-off.

In November, losses continued to hit the squadron with two Fortresses being lost in 134 sorties over seventeen raids. The first of these occurred on the 6th when HB788/B failed to return. It was accompanying a raid to Gravenhorst. None of the ten crewmen survived. Ten days later a tragic accident occurred when HB787/J crashed when attempting to land at Foulsham. The Fortress had been diverted to this airfield because of poor weather over Oulton. The elements were against the crew with a cross wind, a faulty radio transmitter and a cloud base of 100 feet leaving just a few seconds for the pilot to correct his path as needed. The Fortress actually struck the ground several miles from the airfield, bounced and climbed into the cloud, stalled and crashed in a wheat stubble field. It caught fire before any of the crew could escape. The squadron came close to losing a third Fortress in November when HB785/A (F/Sgt D.A. Ingham, RNZAF) was chased by a Me410 (identified as such) on the 30th while covering a raid to Duisburg (576 bombers). The port waist, top and rear gunners opened fire and a big cloud of smoke was seen descending into cloud. The aircraft was therefore claimed as probably destroyed.

December was rather uneventful despite 135 sorties carried out over twenty raids. During the month, the Fortress Mk.IIs were withdrawn with the last sortie on the type flown on the 21st by SR386/Y (F/O Coates). From that point, 214 would be fully operational on the Fortress Mk.III. Because of the generally bad weather conditions in January, the squadron only participated in twelve raids for a total of eighty sorties. The first fortnight was almost uneventful, even though two aircraft had to return with one engine dead due to a technical issue, not the attentions of the enemy. That's what happened to HB796/T (W/O J. Price) on the 7th when the port inner stopped, and to KJ107/N on the 13th (F/O M.C.J. Mark) when the starboard inner caused trouble while orbiting the target. The next night, F/L K. Wyver in HB790/Q (it was the first operational sortie for this aircraft) was attacked by a night fighter around 23.00, after three hours and 20 minutes of flight. The attack was a complete surprise and only noticed by the rear gunner when he sighted green and white tracers coming towards the aircraft from above. Despite that, the German fighter could not be located. Flight Lieutenant Wyver immediately took evasive action to port, but the German night fighter continued its attack unobserved so Wyver continued to take evasive action. The rear gunner decided to open fire in the direction of the source of the tracers in the hope that the German aircraft could at least be scared off. That seems to have been enough for the German night fighter as it ceased its attack. The op, however, had to be abandoned. The Fortress returned and landed at Woodbridge with severe damage: the floor was blown up around the ball turret; a one foot diameter hole in the port wing; and a series of holes along the bottom of the fuselage from tail to mainplane. Fortress HB790 would be out of action, but after repairs it would return to the squadron in May. Two nights later, a tragic accident occurred when KJ103/M crashed near Oulton after hitting a tree on return from an op. One crewmember was killed and six others injured. Operational activity was increased in February with 140 sorties flown that month (18 raids). On the night of 7/8 February, Fortress KJ110/B was attacked by a Ju88 and sustained considerable damage: the H2S and Gee systems were totally destroyed; the nose badly hit; and large holes in

A close-up of the rear mounted Airborne Grocer and Dina aerial used to jam German radars. An American device, it fortunately replaced the Monica tail warning installation when it was found that the German night fighters were able to home in on the Monica transmissions from up to 45 miles away.

When the Fortresses were withdrawn from use, they were sent for storage at 51 MU. Here is KJ122/BU-D with all of its equipment and armament removed. KJ122 had been part of 214 Sqn between 30 March and 22 August 1945.

the starboard mainplane near the rear gunner's compartment. Tragically, the navigator, F/O R.G. Paddick, was severely wounded and died of his wounds the next day. The Special Operator and the waist gunner were also injured, but not severely. The Fortress was repaired and returned to service with 214 after VE-Day. As for the Ju88, it was claimed as destroyed as it was seen to go down in flames. The bad times continued when the next night Fortress HB796/T was posted missing with its entire crew. It had taken off at 21.29 as bomber support for a raid on Krefeld by 151 Lancasters. It was heard to dive into the sea off the British coast with a muffled thud. It seems the pilot attempted to land on the foreshore, but the Fortress bounced and crashed in the sea. There were no survivors. One week later, Fortress HB815/J (F/O S.A. Woods) was attacked by a Ju88, but the combat was short and inconclusive after only a few bursts of gunfire were exchanged. The squadron lost a second Fortress to enemy action in February when HB805/C failed to return on the night 24/25 February. It crashed in German territory with eight crewmembers killed in the crash. A ninth, F/L L.G. Fowler, who had been awarded the DFC while serving with No. 199 Squadron in 1943, was taken prisoner, but would die from his wounds on 15 March. The last crewmember was captured too and spent the last weeks of the war in a PoW camp. This crew was very experienced as it also comprised three DFM holders - F/O J.M. Shorttle, F/O A.M. Jones and F/Sgt G.J.E. Jennings. In March, as the Reich collapsed, Bomber Command maintained its pressure. The squadron participated in twenty raids for a total of 133 sorties in March. Surprisingly, while the Bomber Command squadrons in general saw their losses begin to diminish, 214 would face its worst losses since being a part of 100 Group. The German night fighters were still very active and had re-appeared in the English skies on intruder missions. On 3/4 March, Fortress KJ114/B (F/O R.V. Kingdon, RCAF) was attacked by one of them and returned with holes in the fuselage, one more in the petrol tank, and the pilot's perplex knocked out. Fortress HB802/O (F/O S.A. Woods) was also attacked over Britain, but the intruder missed it and gave up quickly. The Germans were more successful with HB815/J which was shot down by a Ju88 while it was preparing to land and crashed on fire. All on board but two, who were seriously injured, were killed. A few nights later, Fortress KJ106/G was lost over Hamburg as it was shot down by a night fighter while leaving the area. Half of the crew were killed and the other half were captured (some being seriously injured). The next night, HB816/F (W/O J. Price) was also attacked by a night fighter. The waist and mid-upper gunners responded to the attack by opening fire, but the combat was cut short by the Germans who did not press home the attack and broke off. The worst was still to come, however. On the 14/15th, HB802/O failed to return from a bomber support mission over Lutzkendorf. The entire crew became prisoners of war. The next night, HB803/L was attacked by a Ju88 using *Schräge Musik*. The attack started fires in the fuselage and port wing. The rear gunner opened fire and that was enough to drive off the Junkers. The captain, F/O P.J. Anderson, ordered the crew to abandon the aircraft, but two crewmembers failed to do so and were killed. It must be noted that while the Fortress was coming down in flames, an American AA battery fired at it under the impression that it was a Me262. During the same operation, HB799/K returned to base with just the captain, F/L J.G. Wynne, on board! The Fortress was caught by flak and the port inner was hit, caught fire and became uncontrollable. With the danger of the fuel tanks exploding, Wyne ordered his crew to jump. Wyne could not get out and stayed at the controls. The fire eventually began to recede and eventually died out. In the meantime, Wyne had regained control of the Fortress and taken a course to England, preparing to land at the first airfield seen. After half an hour, the engine started to burn again, but this died out again after ten minutes so that only a glow and sparks could be seen. Wyne crossed the Channel and, having found a suitable airfield, circled it and fired the colours of the day. No lights came on so he continued his course for about fifteen minutes. He saw a searchlight, fired a red and orbited while flashing his landing lights. The searchlight gave a bearing which took the aircraft straight over London which was lit up. Wyne altered course and flew until he found an airfield with its lights on. He fired another cartridge, made two circuits and received a green to land. Upon touching down, he felt the left tyre burst. The Fortress ran 1000 yards before it went down on the rim. The propeller of the damaged engine flew off and made a hole in the nose before the aircraft finally stopped. What of his crew? All bailed out over enemy-held territory and, unknown to Wyne, five would later be murdered: Flying Officers Gordon A. Hall, Harold Frost, Sydney C. Matthews, and F/Sgt Edward A. Percival, air gunners, and F/O James W. Vinall, flight engineer. Two more blows would follow within two nights. First, HB785/A was posted missing from the Bohlen operation on the night of 21/22 March. None of the mostly RCAF (American F/O D.N. Donald from Indianapolis was also part of the crew) crew survived. The Hamburg raid claimed KJ112/P and its crew. It was a bittersweet time for the squadron as these would be its last operational losses. Indeed, April was rather uneventful despite 100 sorties being carried out during the month, but it must be said that the Luftwaffe had almost disappeared due to the lack of petrol and the Allies' total air superiority. Only one encounter was made with a German fighter in April (KJ125/J – F/O M. Crosbie on the 4/5th), but no attack was forthcoming. However this crew and plane will live another misfortune soon after when after a mechanical failure, F/O Crosbie was obliged to make a forced landing at Florennes in Belgium returning from mission over Pilsen and Schwandorf during the night 16/17 April. Things continued to go wrong as a sticking throttle finally caused the aircraft the overshoot the runway and to crash. The crew escaped unhurt but KJ125 was struck off charge later in the day. On 2 May, 214 participated in its last wartime operation when it sent eleven Fortresses to Kiel in support of Bomber Command's final raid of the war. In all, the 214 performed 1,280 sorties while flying the Fortress.

Training and flight tests continued and one Fortress was wrecked (HB765/R) on 10 July when the aircraft landed in a rainstorm and ran on to soft ground. The brakes were partially ineffective due to the wet ground and water ingress. HB765 ran off the end of the runway and tipped on its nose before falling back. No one on board was hurt and the Fortress even not seriously damaged was sent to 51 MU for repairs which not not undertaken and HB765 was struck off charge on 10 October. The squadron disbanded on 27 July 1945.

No. 223 Squadron (code 6G):

Number 223 Squadron was the sister squadron of 214 Squadron and was equipped with Liberators handed over by the Americans in the UK and, therefore, beyond the usual Lend-Lease requirements. The squadron was re-formed in August 1944, was also based at Oulton and became operational in September. As with 214's early Fortresses, the Liberators were war-weary, or almost so, USAAF aircraft so their replacement became a necessity by the spring of 1945. As 214 was flying the Fortress from the same airfield, and because the RAF had enough aircraft in reserve at the MUs, it was logical to re-equip 223 with the big Boeing. The first two arrived at the squadron on 16 April (KJ118 and KJ121). While continuing to operate the Liberator, the Fortress was put into action two nights later when KJ118/H, captained by F/L S.B. Mills, participated in a bomber support op with two Liberators. The Fortress had to abandon its

Destined to replace the war-weary Liberators provided by the 8th AF to 223 Sqn, re-equipment had just started when the war ended. Only ten sorties would be flown on Fortresses. Here, seen at 51 MU at Lichfield, is HB793/6G-Q.

task, however, and returned early with the starboard outer stopped. The next night, KJ121/B (F/O G. Bremness, RCAF) was sent out with three Liberators for its baptism of fire. The op was completed without incident. On the night of the 22nd, the two Fortresses returned to operations while, in the meantime, Fortresses KH998, KJ100, KJ113 and KJ115 had been taken on charge. Before the war's end, KJ102, KJ105, KJ117, KJ120 and KJ124 would also be added to the inventory, but 223 would not be fully operational on the type before VE-Day. The last operation carried out took place on the night of 2 May. Nine aircraft being detailed, including four Fortresses. In all, the squadron flew ten sorties on the Fortress. If the war had continued to June, 223 would have been fully operational by the end of that month. With the end of the war, replacing the last Liberators became a low priority and in June the complement of sixteen Fortresses was reached with HB793, HB818, KJ109, KJ110 and possibly KL836 joining the unit. The squadron was disbanded the following month on the 29th.

Claims - 214 Squadron (Confirmed and Probable)

Date	Captain	SN	Origin	Type	Serial	Code	Nb	Cat.
05.06.44	W/C Desmond J. McGlinn	RAF No. 37294	RAF	Me410	**SR386**	BU-N	1.0	C
04.07.44	F/O Thomas J. Bayliss	RAF No. 150250	RAF	Ju88	**SR377**	BU-M	1.0	C
30.11.44	F/Sgt Douglas A. Ingham	NZ427461	RNZAF	Me410	**HB785**	BU-A	1.0	P
07.02.45	W/O Harold Bennett	RAF No. 1531808	RAF	Ju88	**KJ110**	BU-B	1.0	C

Total: 4.0

Summary of the aircraft lost on Operations - 214 Squadron

Date of TO	Crew	S/N	Origin	Serial	Code	Fate
24.05.44	P/O Allan J.N. Hockley	Aus. 420197	RAAF	**SR384**	BU-A	†
	F/Sgt Thomas D. Glenn	RAF No. 1516970	RAF			PoW
	F/Sgt Raoul T. Lyall	Aus. 421541	RAAF			PoW
	F/Sgt Robert Y. Gundy	NZ42663	RNZAF			PoW
	Sgt Raymond G.V. Simpson	RAF No. 1805752	RAF			†
	Sgt Enoch Lovatt	RAF No. 1590361	RAF			PoW
	Sgt Walter W. Hallett	RAF No. 1587281	RAF			PoW
	Sgt James E. McCutchan	Can./ R.178606	RCAF			PoW
	Sgt Robert F. Lloyd-Davis	RAF No. 2211370	RAF			PoW
22.06.44	F/L David M. Peden	Can./ J.20216	RCAF	**SR381**	BU-F	-
	F/Sgt Samuel Mather	RAF No. 1437595	RAF			-
	F/Sgt Alfred Stanley	RAF No. 1147712	RAF			-
	F/O John B. Waters	Can./ J.21576	RCAF			-
	Sgt Albert E. Lester	RAF No. 1873161	RAF			-
	F/Sgt Jack D. Philipps	Aus. 422692	RAAF			-
	Sgt Kenneth W. Bailey	RAF No. 1330826	RAF			-
	F/Sgt John W. Walker	Can./ R.173927	RCAF			-
	F/Sgt Ronald H. Hembrow	Aus. 426840	RAAF			-

	P/O John D. Cassan	RAF No. 172119	RAF	**SR382**	BU-B	†
	F/Sgt George Orr	RAF No. 1551656	RAF			†
	F/Sgt Harry Whatton	RAF No. 1384559	RAF			**PoW**
	W/O Douglas R. Jennings	Can./ R.153179	RCAF			**Evd.**
	Sgt Norman W.S. Abbott	RAF No. 1626469	RAF			†
	F/Sgt Alex Sharpe	RAF No. 1011102	RAF			†
	Sgt Sydney H. Bryant	RAF No. 1851276	RAF			†
	Sgt Thomas S. Sparks	RAF No. 1685161	RAF			**PoW**
	F/Sgt William Milne	RAF No. 1558721	RAF			**PoW**
26.08.44	W/O John R. Lee	RAF No. 1431958	RAF	**HB763**	BU-T	**PoW**
	W/O Gerald H.P. Gibbens	Can./ R.157979	RCAF			**PoW**
	F/Sgt Arthur C. Smith	RAF No. 1092340	RAF			**PoW**
	F/Sgt John E.M. Pitchford	RAF No. 746311	RAF			**PoW**
	Sgt Peter Barkess	RAF No. 1591472	RAF			**PoW**
	Sgt Donald Williamson	RAF No. 1777442	RAF			†
	Sgt Patrick J. Curtis	RAF No. 576549	RAF			**PoW**
	Sgt George Boag	RAF No. 1554282	RAF			†
	Sgt Gordon J.J. Caulfield	RAF No. 1895558	RAF			†
	Sgt Anthony J. McNamara	RAF No. 1582886	RAF			†
12.09.44	F/L Philip R.S. Filleul	RAF No. 33383	RAF	**HB767**	BU-A	†
	P/O Robert L. Dodds	RAF No. 172519	RAF			†
	Sgt Ronnie Birkby	RAF No. 1549729	RAF			†
	F/O Kenneth P. Dack	RAF No. 154246	RAF			†
	Sgt George H. Benson	RAF No. 989053	RAF			†
	Sgt Thomas H. Billington	RAF No. 1044838	RAF			†
	Sgt Patrick J. Wilson	RAF No. 1806740	RAF			†
	Sgt Edwin Dobson	RAF No. 1442409	RAF			†
	Sgt Raymond Cooper	?	RAF			-
	Sgt Jean-Pierre Hanet	RAF No. 1819763	RAF			†
31.10.44	F/Sgt James P. Robertson	NZ422318	RNZAF	**HB800**	BU-V	-
	Sgt A.W. Ramsey	?	RAF			-
	F/Sgt Lionel J. Bennett	NZ42287	RNZAF			-
	F/Sgt Frederick R. Olds	NZ427313	RNZAF			-
	Sgt William T. Banner	RAF No. 2221107	RAF			-
	Sgt William Bunyan	RAF No. 1118147	RAF			-
	Sgt Thomas W.H. Usher	RAF No. 3050447	RAF			-
	Sgt Robert J. Carrott	RAF No. 1816917	RAF			-
	Sgt David C. Nutt	RAF No. 1821172	RAF			-
	Sgt George S.M. Fowler	Aus. 442340	RAAF			-
16.11.44	F/Sgt Colin J. Ashworth	NZ427492	RNZAF	**HB787**	BU-J	†
	Sgt William A. McLaren	RAF No. 1672260	RAF			†
	F/Sgt Ernest R. Armstrong	NZ427084	RNZAF			†
	Sgt Peter E. Durman	RAF No. 1389300	RAF			†
	F/Sgt Alexander McLaughlin	NZ422972	RNZAF			†
	F/Sgt Terence F. McCormack	NZ429183	RNZAF			†
	Sgt Gilbert L. Hislop	RAF No. 1594952	RAF			†
	Sgt Richard E. Mooney	Can./ R.261225	RCAF			†
	Sgt Charles G.M. Ogivie	RAF No. 621667	RAF			†
	P/O Archibald H. Leitch	Can./ J.44328	RCAF			†
16.01.45	F/O Neil T. Scott	RAF No. 152592	RAF	**KJ103**	BU-M	-
	F/O Robert V. Houston	Can./ J.37516	RCAF			-
	Sgt David V. Lewis	RAF No. 1083677	RAF			-
	F/O Terrence V. McKee	Can./ J.37516	RCAF			†
	F/Sgt Richard S. Smith	RAF No. 1812297	RAF			-
	Sgt Bernard J. F. Lunn	RAF No. 1895893	RAF			-
	Sgt Richard J. Willing	RAF No. 1896166	RAF			-
	Sgt Cecil Brown	RAF No. 1892486	RAF			-
	F/Sgt Robert J. Knickle	Can./ R.213050	RCAF			-

Date	Name	Service No.	Air Force	Aircraft	Code	Fate
	F/O Eric T. Hardman	Aus. 424832	RAAF			-
08.02.45	P/O James P. Roberston	NZ422318	RNZAF	HB796	BU-T	†
	F/Sgt Peter G. Buckland	RAF No. 1337316	RAF			†
	W/O Lionel J. Bennett	NZ42287	RNZAF			†
	F/Sgt Frederick R. Olds	NZ427313	RNZAF			†
	Sgt William T. Banner	RAF No. 2221107	RAF			†
	Sgt William Bunyan	RAF No. 1118147	RAF			†
	Sgt Thomas W.H. Usher	RAF No. 3050447	RAF			†
	Sgt Robert J. Carrott	RAF No. 1816917	RAF			†
	Sgt Ernest Dobson	RAF No. 1590215	RAF			†
	Sgt George S.M. Fowler	Aus. 442340	RAAF			†
24.02.45	F/O Josph M. Shortlle	RAF No. 157422	RAF	HB805	BU-C	†
	F/L Leslie G. Fowler	RAF No. 126036	RAF			†
	W/O Francis H. Dix	NZ411069	RNZAF			†
	W/O Richard W. Towell	RAF No. 977635	RAF			†
	F/O Allan M. Jones	RAF No. 178636	RAF			†
	F/Sgt Geoffrey J.E. Jennings	RAF No. 1394514	RAF			PoW
	F/O Frank R. Woodger	RAF No. 52114	RAF			†
	Sgt Thomas W.J. Pollard	RAF No. 1865782	RAF			†
	F/Sgt Stanley L. Jones	RAF No. 1256275	RAF			†
	P/O Kenneth C. Allan	RAF No. 183538	RAF			†
03.03.45	F/O Harry Bennett	RAF No. 190245	RAF	HB815	BU-J	†
	F/Sgt Harry Barnfield	RAF No. 1059973	RAF			†
	F/Sgt William Briddon	RAF No. 1817057	RAF			†
	Sgt Frank Hares	RAF No. 1581827	RAF			†
	F/Sgt Leslie A. Hadder	RAF No. 1804649	RAF			†
	Sgt Patrick J. Healy	RAF No. 1300369	RAF			†
	Sgt Leslie E. Billington	RAF No. 2205644	RAF			†
	Sgt Alastair McDermid	RAF No. 2202207	RAF			-
	W/O Ronald W. Church	RAF No. 636466	RAF			-
	W/O Lindsay J. Odgers	Aus. 417595	RAAF			†
07.03.45	F/O George Stewart	NZ421849	RNZAF	KJ106	BU-G	†
	Sgt Hugh McC. McClymont	RAF No. 1681945	RAF			†
	F/Sgt John V. Matthews	Aus. 428920	RAAF			PoW
	F/Sgt John W. Winstone	NZ429389	RNZAF			†
	W/O John Henderson	RAF No. 960250	RAF			PoW
	F/Sgt Harry L. Henderson	Can./ R.211939	RCAF			†
	Sgt William P. Mulhall	RAF No. 2210752	RAF			PoW
	Sgt Alan A. Goldstone	RAF No. 1051488	RAF			PoW
	Sgt Kenneth C. Phelan	RAF No. 2223209	RAF			PoW
	F/O Nicholas Peters	Can./ J.45525	RCAF			†
14.03.45	F/L Norman Rix	RAF No. 152473	RAF	HB802	BU-O	PoW
	P/O Hartley T. Sargeant	Aus. 419278	RAAF			PoW
	W/O Albert R. Irvine	Aus. 421277	RAAF			PoW
	F/O William J. Lovell-Smith	NZ425950	RNZAF			PoW
	F/Sgt Jopseph L. Cuttance	NZ4215732	RNZAF			PoW
	F/Sgt Russell O. Douglas	NZ4211646	RNZAF			PoW
	Sgt Leonard J. Pound	RAF No. 1894471	RAF			PoW
	Sgt Raymond Gamble	RAF No. 1869889	RAF			PoW
	Sgt Brian Burgess	RAF No. 2204386	RAF			PoW
	F/Sgt Alexander D. Mackintosh	RAF No. 1875517	RAF			PoW
15.03.45	F/O Peter J. Anderson	RAF No. 169080	RAF	HB803	BU-L	-
	F/O Frank J.A.W. Burnett	RAF No. 173289	RAF			-
	W/O Maurice C. White	RAF No. 1166191	RAF			†
	P/O John A. Morton	RAF No. 173162	RAF			-
	F/Sgt H.T. Harmsworth	?	RAF			-
	W/O J. Hunter	?	RAF			-
	F/Sgt George A. Mercer	RAF No. 1536654	RAF			-

Date	Crew	S/N	Origin	Serial	Code	Fate
	W/O Leslie T. **Wheeler**	RAF No. 1397442	RAF			-
	F/O Jacques E. **Cryer**	RAF No. 141282	RAF			†
20.03.45	F/O Robert V. **Kingdon**	Can./ J.28299	RCAF	**HB785**	BU-A	†
	F/Sgt William A. **Routley**	Can./ R.179830	RCAF			†
	F/Sgt Donald F. **Miller**	RAF No. 1809260	RAF			†
	W/O James W. **Pellant**	Can./ R.147701	RCAF			†
	F/Sgt Hilton M. **Carter**	Can./ R.253380	RCAF			†
	W/O Robert G. **Wilson**	Can./ R.197780	RCAF			†
	Sgt William D. **Dale**	RAF No. 1594366	RAF			†
	Sgt Walter **Perkins**	RAF No. 2223326	RAF			†
	F/O Douglas N. **Donald**	Can./ J.47071	(US)/RCAF			†
21.03.45	F/L William D. **Allies**	RAF No. 41978	RAF	**KJ112**	BU-P	†
	F/O Brian F. **Kerr**	RAF No. 148842	RAF			†
	F/O Stafford H.G. **Sinclair**	RAF No. 178092	RAF			†
	P/O Wilfred J. **Cunningham**	RAF No. 149252	RAF			†
	F/Sgt Charles R.W. **Braithwaite**	RAF No. 1812034	RAF			†
	Sgt Peter **Newman**	RAF No. 1816804	RAF			†
	Sgt James **McFarlane**	RAF No. 994024	RAF			†
	Sgt Robert A.D. **Jones**	RAF No. 1811322	RAF			†
	Sgt Edward L. **Punnett**	RAF No. 1606932	RAF			†
	W/O Norman **Cooper**	RAF No. 916151	RAF			†
16.04.45	F/L Michael **Crosbie**	RAF No. 186368	RAF	**KJ125**	BU-J	-
	F/O Douglas W. **Hall**	Can./ J.39949	RCAF			-
	F/Sgt Brian L. **Collings**	RAF No. 548543	RAF			-
	F/O John W. **Carter**	Can./J.37715	RCAF			-
	Sgt S.G. **Edwards**	?	RAF			-
	F/Sgt Donald E. **Astbury**	RAF No. 1661561	RAF			-
	Sgt Walter G. **Mercer**	RAF No. 1880522	RAF			-
	Sgt William J. **Heath**	RAF No. 2287236	RAF			-
	Sgt T. **Sullivan**	?	RAF			-
	F/O Stephen **Nessner**	Can./ J.45404	RCAF			-

Total: 17

Summary of the aircraft lost by accident - 214 Squadron

Date	Crew	S/N	Origin	Serial	Code	Fate
10.07.45	F/O Kenneth W. **Spencer** *Rest of the crew not known but no casualty reported.*	RAF No. 170120	RAF	**HB765**	BU-R	-

Total: 1

FORTRESS B. MK.III
CYCLONE
AUGUST 1944

Fortress HB796 after the fitting of all of its operational equipment. It was later issued to 214 Sqn as BU-T on 06.09.44 and carried out its first sortie the following 27 September. It was posted missing on 7/8 February 1945.

With the RCAF

In 1943, the need to deliver mail to Canadian servicemen in the UK had become a huge task. The RCAF had no choice but to organise something much better than the service in place at the time. It created a full squadron to be dedicated to the task. Therefore, No. 168 (Heavy Transport) Squadron was formed on 18 October 1943 at Rockliffe (Ottawa, Canada). While the squadron took deliveries of Lockheed Lodestars, they were not used for very long. To make the Atlantic crossing, the squadron needed long-range aircraft and only the B-24 Liberator or the B-17 Flying Fortress could be considered. Training was, however, conducted on the Lodestars while pilots, wireless operators and navigators spent time at Dorval (Quebec) for instructions and briefing by 45 Group HQ on transatlantic operations. In the meantime, the RCAF obtained the release of six B-17s from the AAF training units after the personal intervention of General H.H. Arnold. The B-17s consisted of three E models (41-9142, 41-2438, 41-2581) and three F models (42-3160, 42-6101, 42-3369). On 26 November, two pilots, two co-pilots and two wireless operators proceeded to Lockbourne Army Air Base in Ohio to be trained on the B-17. When completed, the first B-17F headed to Canada on 4 December. The other two B-17Fs arrived on 5 December and 8 December respectively and the three received the serials 9202, 9203 and 9204. As those B-17s had previously been used as trainers in the USA, they were already lacking turrets and armour plating, so there was little to be done in the way of modifications to carry the mail overseas. The only additions were a series of small auxiliary fuel tanks, known as 'Tokyo tanks', in the outer wings which gave about six and a half hours flying time in addition to the nine hour endurance from the main tanks. The training and planning of the flights continued over the following days and the first crossing was scheduled for 14 December with a load of Christmas mail. However, the two Fortresses ready for the first run developed engine trouble and the run was cancelled. Worse, 9202 had an engine reduction gear failure which meant that an entire engine had to be changed. The 'great day' came the next day when, at 14.22, Fortress 9204 left Rockcliffe for the first flight of the RCAF overseas airmail service, or 'Mailcan' as it was to be known within the RCAF. The CO, W/C R.B. Middleton was in command. The load consisted of 189 bags of mail weighing a total of 5502 pounds. The trip consisted of stops at Dorval (Montreal), Gander and eventually Prestwick in Scotland. In the meantime, the first B-17E had arrived in Canada on the 13th and would be followed by a second on the 19th. They were given serials 9205 and 9206. The last of the three B-17Es would finally arrive on 1 February 1944 and would become 9207.

The first aircraft to return to Rockcliffe was 9202 on 10 January with 1,400,000 letters from overseas. Fortress 9203 arrived the next day. Both had landed in the UK, Morocco, Algeria, Tunisia, Libya, Egypt, Malta, Italy and Gibraltar before returning to Canada. By the end of February 1944 the squadron was well organised for the duty it had been formed for with Fortresses doing the long legs while Dakotas used by the squadron were taking care of the short runs. In spring, the North Atlantic route was gradually phased out in favour of a route staging though the airfield of Lagens in the Azores with Gibraltar becoming the first European landing. The Fortresses were

The crew that performed the first mailrun with a Fortress - P/O E.M. Rosenbaum, F/L B.G. Smith, F/O C.A. Dickson and F.B. Labrish - standing in front of the B-17F (42-6101) that became 9203.

Fortress 9203 seen at Rockliffe with five mailbags painted on its nose.

extensively used through 1944 and the flights remained a dangerous task. On 2 April 1944, 9207 crashed at Prestwick just after it had taken off. It was seen to climb very steeply, turn sharply to the left and spin in. The five crewmembers were killed. No definite cause for the accident was determined, but it was thought probable that the crash was due to the cargo shifting.

The use of the Fortresses was a temporary measure while awaiting the delivery of eighteen C-87s from the USA. This, however, never took place because of the type's lack of availability. Therefore, the RCAF had to divert B-24 Liberators for transport duty and the first three arrived at the squadron on 1 August. As they were unmodified, the Fortresses had to continue to make the 'Mailcan' alone, while the demand for the service increased with the invasion of the Continent from June 1944. Things got worse the following month when the undercarriage of 9204 collapsed after landing at Rockcliffe. None of the crew was injured, but damage was such that the aircraft

Mailbags being unloaded into Fortress 9204, not an easy task seeing how the groundcrews have to proceed. The Fortress was a bomber and was chosen for its endurance, but was not really suited to carry anything other than bombs. All the attempts to convert the B-17 into a transport aircraft, carrying passengers or conventional loads, failed. The B-24 was more successful in this role.

41

had to be written off. In October, the Liberators gradually became available to reinforce the Fortresses in their task, but the number of Fortresses was cut by one on 15 December when 9203 and her crew were posted missing between Rabat Sale, in Morocco, and Lagens. Some floating mailbags were picked up by a British destroyer four days later about 100 miles from Lagens. The end of the war didn't mean the end of the 'Mailcan', as Canadian troops were still stationed in Europe, so the Fortresses soldiered on. The squadron was sometimes asked to carry loads besides the mail such as in late October 1945 when the RCAF was called upon to rush desperately required supplies of penicillin from Canada to Warsaw. The Fortresses were chosen for this type of operation and Russian permission was obtained for the flight to Poland. Fortress 9205 carried out its task successfully, but Fortress 9202 crashed near Munster in Germany on 4 November 1945 and all five on board were killed.

At the beginning of 1946, with the reduction of the number of Canadian personnel in Europe and the increasing civil air traffic across the Atlantic able to handle mail transport, the days of 168 Squadron were numbered. It disbanded on 21 March. The Fortresses had completed 240 transatlantic flights since the service had begun. The remaining aircraft were dispersed for storage. Fortress 9202 had already been written off the previous month and 9206 met the same fate in June. Fortress 9205 was to serve briefly with No. 9 (Transport) Group's Air Sea Rescue, but was eventually written off on 27 December 1946. Fortress 9205 and 9206 would eventually continue a civil career in Argentina.

Summary of the aircraft lost by accident - 168 Squadron RCAF

Date	Crew	S/N	Origin	Serial	Code	Fate
02.04.44	F/O Norman C. Cathcart	Can./ C.6248	(us)/RCAF	9207		†
	F/O John D. Shanahan	Can./ J.16166	(us)/RCAF			†
	F/O Hugh C. McFadden	Can./ J.14632	RCAF			†
	F/O Gordon T. Gaunt	Can./ J.14910	RCAF			†
	Cpl Elmer I. Lavergne	Can./ R.156555	RCAF			†
17.09.44	F/L William G. Proudfoot	Can./ C.6727	RCAF	9204		-
	F/O Norman L. Martin	Can./ J.47542	RCAF			-
	F/L Charles R. Gates	Can./ C.1835	RCAF			-
	P/O William A.R. McDonald	Can./ J.46745	RCAF			-
	Cpl Ernest E. Morin	Can./ R.94009	RCAF			-
15.12.44	F/L Horace B. Hillcoat	Can./ C.21305	RCAF	9203		†
	F/L Alfred JdeL. Ruttledge	Can./ J.15160	RCAF			†
	F/L Frederick B. La Brish	Can./ J.4763	RCAF			†
	F/O Cecil A. Dickson	Can./ J.10870	RCAF			†
	Cpl Robert E. Bruce	Can./ R.192653	RCAF			†
	*F/L William S. Pullar**	Can./ J.18049	RCAF			†
	*F/L Douglas H. Sharpe**	Can./ J.11485	RCAF			†
	*F/L William L. Wilson**	Can./ C.12659	RCAF			†
04.11.45	F/L Edward P. Harling	Can./ J.4331	RCAF	9202		†
	F/L Donald F. Caldwell	Can./ J.11098	RCAF			†
	S/L Alfred E. Webster	Can./ J.4956	RCAF			†
	F/L Norbert Roche	Can./ J.15269	RCAF			†
	Sgt Edwin E. Phillips	Can./ R.174196	RCAF			†

Total: 4

*Passengers

At the end of their career, the RCAF Fortresses were deeply modified especially in the nose area where a cargo space was installed. Accessible from the nose itself, the space was not glazed (fabric covered) and could be opened. It was strong enough to serve as a loading platform.

Fortress 9205 seen while taxiing at Rockliffe immediately after the war. This aircraft was one of the last two Canadian Fortresses operational in 1946 (the other was 9206) and they received the codes QA and QB painted on the nose.

With miscellaneous units

While being withdrawn from combat units, the Fortress began to be used to fulfil another key role in the Meteorological squadrons. Accurate weather forecasts had become part of the preparation for operations at the end of WW2. For this, oceanic systems had to be studied and long-range aircraft were needed. Towards the end of the war, six 'Met' squadrons had been formed, three of them would receive Fortresses as equipment - Nos. 251, 519 and 521 Squadrons. The first to receive the Fortress was 519 based at Wick. It was also equipped with various other aircraft types, including the Spitfire Mk.VI and Mk.VII (see SQUADRONS! No. 1 and SQUADRONS! No. 6). The first Fortress to arrive at the squadron was FL455/A in mid-November 1944 and the first Met flight was carried out on the 26th and lasted four hours. In December, it was joined by FL450/D and FA695/C on the 2nd, then by FL464/B, FA696/J, FA712/E, FL449/F and FK213/G respectively. In January, FK211/H joined the fleet. At that time, a typical crew comprised eight or nine men. The squadron was flying two types of sorties. The RECIPE sortie extended northwards beyond the Artic Circle and was flown twice each day with takeoffs planned around midday (RECIPE I) and midnight (RECIPE II). The RHOMBUS sortie was a two-leg operation out over the North Sea to a point 100 miles southwest of Kristiansand in Norway. The operational start for the Fortress was low-key, but full operational status would be achieved by mid-March 1945. In the meantime, the squadron suffered a dramatic event with the loss of FL455/A and its crew on 2 February. The Fortress had taken off from Wick at 10.45 on a RECIPE I Met flight. On the return flight, the weather became very bad with gusting snowstorms and low cloud to the point that all other flying had been cancelled. The Fortress iced up and its radio altimeter failed. The captain, F/L Keith 'Bluey' Humphreys reported having trouble with the carburetor icing controls. At 20.40, while circling to find the airfield, the Fortress flew into level, marshy terrain near Halsary, some twelve miles from Wick. It slid along the surface and broke in two. Four men were killed in the crash, and the survivors, two being badly injured, were rescued the following day. Sadly, the two injured aircrew would die within two days. The squadron continued its task until the end of June 1945 when the last Met flight was recorded, a flight carried out by S/L Gerry Chandler in FL459/M. It was actually an abrupt and unexpected end as corrosion had been found in a tailplane spar during an inspection. All of the squadron's fleet was grounded and the ban was lifted on 12 July. It must be said that these Fortresses had been extensively used over the previous three years. The squadron's role was initially undertaken by Halifaxes from 518 Squadron and, in July it was decided to convert 519 to the Halifax. With the war in Europe over, a number of near new Halifax IIIs became available and they were in far better shape than the old Fortress IIs and IIAs. In all, 519 flew close to 2,750 hours on Met flights in over 300 sorties.

The second Met squadron to operate the Fortress was No. 521 Squadron, based at Langham, and, at the time of the changeover, was using the Hudson for long-range sorties. Preparations started in December using a Fortress from 1674 HCU (FL463) for training and the first Fortresses allocated to 521 arrived at the squadron, FA703 and FA710, on the 18th followed by FL456 four days later. Fortress FL452 arrived early in February 1945 and the first sorties were carried on the 27th. Until May, the squadron used these Fortresses which were reinforced by FK210 and FL450 in May. In June, 521 took charge of its only Fortress Mk.III (HB786). In November, the squadron moved to Chivenor after having flown more than 350 Met flights from Langham. From Chivenor, about fifty more Met flights would be performed until 8 January 1946. That day, Fortress FA703 took off with F/O Peter M. Williams in

Fortress FL464/AD-E of 251 Sqn at Reykjavik during the summer of 1945. This Fortress, with all of its turrets and armament removed, served with the squadron between August and December 1945. The codes are black. *(via Robert M. Stitt)*

command. Soon after, he experienced an RPM fluctuation from the starboard inner engine. The situation returned to normal, then later on the RPM dropped seriously while the oil temperature began to rise. Williams asked his co-pilot to feather the propeller, but the propeller of the starboard outer engine was feathered instead. Now with one engine dead and another unable to give sufficient power, the Fortress began to lose height. Unable to regain control, Williams decided to ditch. It was a ditching that only three crewmembers would survive. Because of this incident, the Fortresses, the last operational in the RAF, were grounded and conversion to the Halifax, which had begun in December, accelerated, marking a sad end to the career of the Fortress in RAF service.

The third and last Met unit to use the Fortress was No. 251 Squadron. Based at Reykjavik in Iceland, it had a dual mission of Met flights and ASR duties. The first two Fortresses to be issued to the squadron were FK184 and FK185. These were used to convert the crews to the big Boeing. In April and May, seven more Fortresses were taken on charge (FK196 on 1 April, FL451 on 13 April, FL451 on 2 May, FK197 on 3 May, FK203 on 19 May, and FA701 and FK194 on 30 May). In all, and until the end of summer 1945,

Fortress II FA695/Z9-C of 519 Sqn seen at Wick in the spring of 1945. Even though only used for Met flights, the Fortress is still armed, but the chances of encountering a German aircraft were almost non-existent at the time. *(via Robert M. Stitt)*

45

Fortress FK197/AD-E served for two and a half years with Scottish Aviation dedicated to LRASV radar trials. It flew with 251 Sqn between May and the end of July 1945 and was eventually replaced by FL464 (see previous page).

Fortress FK205/D of 1674 HCU at Aldergrove in 1945. This Fortress was to be a part of this unit for a long time (between January 1944 and September 1945) before it was sent for storage at 51 MU. (via Robert M. Stiit)

251 would see seventeen Fortresses, including two Mk.IIIs (HB791 and HB792). The first Met sortie was on 3 May with FL451 flown by F/L A.G. Frandsen and crew of seven. The op was called MAGNUM, a standard sortie of an out-and-return, with a radius of 650 miles (over 1,000 km), southwest of Reykjavik over the Altantic. The normal total time of a typical sortie was around eight hours. Later, this kind of sortie would be extended to a triangular track that could be flown clockwise or anti-clockwise. The squadron continued to operate until being disbanded on 30 October after having performed 725 hours on Fortresses over 85 sorties. During its service with 251, only one Fortress fell victim to an accident - FL451 was damaged when it ran off the end of the runway. No attempt was made to repair it and it was eventually struck off charge on 29 May 1946.

Because of the small number of Fortresses available for the operational units, only a few Fortress IIs or IIIs were assigned to training units. Number 1 (Coastal) OTU, in charge of training crews for Coastal Command, received only three Fortresses (FK196, FK199 and FL450) and this was only for a short time from the end of August 1943. Indeed, the first two left the unit at the end of October and FL450 followed two weeks later. All three were re-assigned to No. 1674 HCU which had been formed on 10 October to provide conversion training for crews intended for long-range patrol squadrons. The initial equipment was established with five Fortresses, as far as the type was concerned, initially from 1 OTU and the full complement was in place by January 1944. This training ceased in September 1944, but was resumed in December only to be halted for good in August 1945. The initial establishment was slightly increased in 1944 and two Mk.IIIs (HB776 and HB778) were added in April and May 1944, but were sent to 51 MU when training ceased in September. Only one accident was

Photo of Fortresses from the RWE are rare, but at least we have proof of their presence at the unit. Here two crewmembers are posing in the upper hatch of the Fortress and allow us to see the codes 'U3'. Note that we can guess the previous unit, 223 Sqn, as the codes '6G' have been painted over. It is believed that this Fortress is KJ117/U3-E. (via Andrew Thomas)

Among the various trials conducted on the Fortress by the A&AEE, FK185 was fitted with a Vickers 40mm 'S' gun in the nose section. The letter 'E' on the nose is not an individual letter from the A&AEE, but the remnants of its previous owner, 220 Sqn. We can distinguish the full codes (NR-E) that have been painted over on either side of the roundel. The trials were proved to be satisfactory, but the concept never went beyond the prototype phase.

recorded when, on 22 June 1945, FK201 left the runway at Aldergrove (the station where 1674 was based) after an engine took fire. The aircraft was not repaired.

Bomber Command had its own training flight too since the re-introduction of the type in 1944. To train crews for 214 (and 223 with its Liberators), No. 1699 Flight was formed on 24 April 1944 (re-designated 1699 HCU on 24 October). It was disbanded on 29 June 1945. Initially, some Fortress Mk.Is were taken on charge. In all seven Fortress IIs or IIIs would serve with the flight, flight which relocated at Oulton to get closer to No. 214 Squadron. The first Fortresses to be officially issued to the flight were on 8 December (SR383, SR386 and SR388) but it is believed that they were already on use since August as aircraft X, Y and Z. They were occasionally used in operations to reinforce No. 214 Squadron until the end of 1944. In spring 1945, four former 214 Squadron Fortress Mk.IIIs (HB793, HB818, KJ104 and KJ109) arrived to replace the ageing ex-USAAF Fortress IIs. During the type's time with the flight, two Fortresses were involved in accidents. The first occurred on 12 September 1944 when SR380 crashed on landing. On loan from 214, it tipped on its nose and one of the air gunners was injured. The second accident involved SR386 when it hit trees on approach and crashed when returning from a night training flight. The crash occurred when the pilot was temporarily blinded following the explosion of a flare fired by Flying Control.

Regarding units not involved in training duties, the A&AEE and the RAE (Royal Aircraft Establishment) were in charge of testing the type. The first used five Mk.IIs and three Mk.IIIs and the latter five Mk.IIs and two Mk.IIIs, the last of these were used until the spring of 1946. Among the aircraft tested by the A&AEE was FK185 which was fitted with a 40mm cannon in its nose. It would begin a second career when it was issued to 251 Squadron in March 1945. FK187 spent most its career as a test aircraft and was never issued to any operational unit, as was FK192 which was used for high altitude flights and meteorological research. Fortress FK211 was used to test IFF equipment and for gun trials and would eventually be issued to 206 Squadron in August 1943. Only one Fortress II was used for testing. FA706 flew astrodome trials between December 1942 and April 1943 before it was issued to 220 Squadron. At the end of the war in 1945, two Mk.IIIs would be used for a short time (HB776 and KL835).

The Radio Warfare Establishment (RWE) also used a number of Fortresses. Formed on 21 July 1945 at Swanton Morley, it was part of Bomber Command's 100 Group. Its aircraft used the codes 'U3'. About eight Fortress IIIs were taken on charge during the summer (KJ100, KJ102, KJ105, KJ113, KJ115, KJ118 and KJ120) and all were issued on 9 August. The unit's tasks were to conduct electronic warfare and operate radio countermeasures. Its main activities were divided between intelligence gathering and radar jamming. The Fortress was the perfect platform for this task, but, with the end of the Lend-Lease system, the type was withdrawn between March and June 1946. In the same vein, it must be noted that one Fortress, SR385, was also used by the TFU (Telecommunication Flying Unit) in the development of radio equipment and techniques. It was used between August 1945 and March 1946 before being sent to storage for the same reasons as the aircraft used by the RWE.

Summary of the aircraft lost on Operations - Other units

Date	Pilot and crew when known	S/N	Origin	Serial	Code	Unit	Fate
12.09.44	F/O Marc C.J. Stainier	RAF No. 157938	(BEL)/RAF	SR380		1699 HCU	-
	Rest of the crew not reported but safe.						-
01.02.45	F/L Frederick K. Humphreys	RAF No. 84673	RAF	FL455	Z9-A	519 Sqn	-
	F/L Edwin A. Wood*	RAF No. 109926	RAF				†
	F/O George H. Pullan	RAF No. 151496	RAF				-
	F/O Thomas G. Wrigley	RAF No. 153955	RAF				-
	F/Sgt Geoffrey A. Panzer	RAF No. 1384480	RAF				†
	F/Sgt Kenneth A. Day	RAF No. 1234239	RAF				†
	F/Sgt William H. Payne	RAF No. 1738660	RAF				†
	Sgt Alexander P. Beatson	RAF No. 823242	RAF				†
	Sgt Dennis A. Pressley	RAF No. 1640545	RAF				†
06.04.45	F/O Edward R. Carter	RAF No. 51728	RAF	SR386		1699 HCU	-
	Rest of the crew not reported but safe.						-
22.06.45	F/Sgt George A. Tough	RAF No. 1567428	RAF	FK201		1674 HCU	-
	Rest of the crew not reported but safe.						
29.08.45	W/O Edward G. Melville	RAF No. 1814007	RAF	FL451	AD-A	251 Sqn	-
	Rest of the crew not reported but safe.						
08.01.46	F/O Peter M. Williams	RAF No. 198318	RAF	FA703		521 Sqn	-
	F/Sgt Victor C. Taylor	RAF No. 1801093	RAF				-
	F/O George B. Sharp	RAF No. 164868	RAF				†
	W/O Peter W. Collett	RAF No. 1604803	RAF				-
	F/O Reginald G. Cummings	RAF No. 56649	RAF				†
	F/Sgt James K. Thrower	RAF No. 1435458	RAF				†
	W/O Edgar S. Newark	RAF No. 1331073	RAF				†
	Sgt David T. Brown	RAF No. 3031563	RAF				†

*Died of injuries on 12.02.45

Total: 6

Flying Officer Marc Stainier was one and possibly the only non-Commonwealth or American citizen to have served in a operational Fortress squadron. He served before the war in the Belgian military aviation and was captured by the Germans on 28 May 1940; he managed to escape two weeks later and returned home. He later left Belgium in the aim to join the RAF but was interned in Spain in November 1942 during his journey. He would be freed in April 1943 and reached the UK at the end of July 1943. After the usual security procedures, he was authorised to join the RAF and enlisted in October 1943. He was re-trained and elected to undertake a heavy bomber training course and in July 1944 he was ready to go to a Lancaster squadron as a pilot when the plan changed and he went for a Fortress conversion course in September instead (1699 HCU). At the end of September he was posted to No. 214 Squadron. However for security reasons, he prefered to change his name in case of capture and after a couple of missions, he would appear as Flying Officer MCJ Mark. It would be under that name that he received the DFC in September 1945. He left the RAF in December 1945 to join the Belgian airline SABENA.

(André Bar)

End of the road for RAF Fortresses. The USAAF had so many B-17s in their storage facilities in Europe or in the US that surviving Fortresses were never requested to be returned by the Americans and were left on open storage for many months awaiting for their final fate.
Here we can see, at 51 MU of Lichfield, FL463/C, formerly of 1674 HCU, and HB792/AD-D, of 251 Sqn.

Known time of operational use
Flying Units (except trial units)

Serials		Date on Sqn	Date off Sqn	Nbr of sorties	Op Hours flown	Sorties/Hours
FA695:	206 Sqn [V]	28.06.43	31.03.44	21	226.3	
	519 Sqn [Z9-C]	02.12.44	17.09.45	44	385.7	**65/612.0**
FA696:	206 Sqn [Y]	28.06.43	31.03.44	33	309.5	
	519 Sqn [Z9-J]	12.12.44	01.08.45	8	54.9	
	251 Sqn	01.08.45	19.11.45	2	17.8	
	521 Sqn [B]	19.11.45	15.02.46	7	80.2	**50/462.4**
FA697:	220 Sqn [T]	26.08.43	19.12.43	3	23.9	**3/23.9**
FA698:	59 Sqn [V]	12.03.43	26.03.43	2	20.8	**5/20.8**
FA699:	206 Sqn [O]	08.07.43	31.03.44	32	339.2	
	220 Sqn [K]	??.05.44	23.12.44	42	478.0	
	519 Sqn [Z9-L]	03.02.45	24.07.45	20	179.3	
	251 Sqn	24.07.45	22.12.45	3	29.2	**97/1025.7**
FA700:	206 Sqn [R]	27.06.43	31.03.44	33	327.8	
	220 Sqn [R]	17.06.44	18.12.44	28	319.9	
	519 Sqn [Z9-K]	03.02.45	20.07.45	26	255.9	
	251 Sqn	20.07.45	22.12.45	4	34.6	**91/938.2**
FA701:	220 Sqn [F]	15.07.43	16.01.45	77	818.7	
	251 Sqn [AD-J]	30.05.45	08.01.46	11	97.1	**88/915.8**
FA702:	206 Sqn [P]	12.04.43	27.08.43	23	204.9	
	1674 HCU	23.04.43	05.09.45	-	-	**23/204.9**
FA703:	59 Sqn [T]	28.02.43	18.04.43	6	66.4	
	206 Sqn [A]	18.04.43	29.07.43	11	107.5	
	1674 HCU	18.01.44	15.05.44	-	-	
	519 Sqn	30.12.44	18.01.45	-	-	
	521 Sqn	18.01.45	08.01.46	78	510.4	**89/617.9**
FA704:	59 Sqn [R]	07.03.43	17.04.43	5	53.7	
	206 Sqn [R]	17.04.43	11.06.43	9	77.1*	**14/130.8***
FA705:	206 Sqn [O]	27.03.43	24.06.43	8	80.1	
	206 Sqn [U]	25.10.43	06.01.44	13	120.0*	**21/200.1***
FA706:	220 Sqn [S]	10.04.43	02.08.44	41	434.4	**41/434.4**
FA707:	206 Sqn [S]	27.07.43	31.03.44	28	317.0	
	220 Sqn [Z]	14.06.44	26.07.44	2	8.1*	**43/442.5***
FA708:	206 Sqn	10.02.43	23.06.43	-	-	
	220 Sqn [D]	23.06.43	30.11.43	9	72.3	**9/72.3**
FA709:	220 Sqn [B]	17.04.43	03.02.42	2	12.1	
	220 Sqn [A]	25.10.43	18.12.44	61	689.3	**63/701.4**
FA710:	206 Sqn [M]	05.07.43	19.03.44	26	240.3	
	220 Sqn [M]	19.03.44	09.12.44	38	437.5	
	521 Sqn	18.01.45	29.01.46	66	387.2	**130/1065.0**
FA711:	206 Sqn [E]	20.07.43	20.02.44	30	315.8	**30/315.8**
FA712:	519 Sqn [Z9-E]	22.12.44	26.07.45	23	219.4	
	251 Sqn [AD-C]	26.07.45	08.01.45	4	26.1	**27/245.5**
FA713:	220 Sqn	23.07.43	29.07.43	-	-	
	206 Sqn	29.07.43	08.11.43	-	-	
	220 Sqn [E]	08.11.43	12.04.45	74	862.3	**74/862.3**
FK184:	206 Sqn [K]	14.08.42	07.04.44	-	-	
	251 Sqn [AD-A]	11.03.45	05.06.45	-	-	-
FK185:	220 Sqn [E]	14.07.42	31.01.44	14	115.6	
	251 Sqn	11.03.45	30.05.45	-	-	**14/115.6**
FK186:	220 Sqn [S]	23.07.42	23.06.43	45	396.7	
	206 Sqn [X]	12.08.43	19.03.44	7	78.7	
	220 Sqn [X]	19.03.44	15.12.44	35	417.5	**87/892.9**
FK187:	-	-	-	-	-	-

51

FK188:	59 Sqn	15.12.42	29.05.43	-	-	
	220 Sqn [Z]	20.08.43	27.07.44	26	302.7	
	220 Sqn	15.09.44	18.12.44	-	-	
	519 Sqn	20.02.45	23.03.45	-	-	**26/302.7**
FK189:	59 Sqn [S]	11.06.43	21.04.43	-	-	
	220 Sqn [Y from 03.44]	26.08.43	27.07.44	4	49.2	**4/49.2**
FK190:	206 Sqn [J]	18.03.43	27.04.44	6	49.1	
	220 Sqn	27.04.44	08.06.44	-	-	**6/49.1**
FK191:	206 Sqn [N]	13.09.42	29.04.43	-	-	
	220 Sqn [P]	09.08.43	18.12.44	46	515.3	**46/515.3**
FK192:	-	-	-	-	-	-
FK193:	220 Sqn [H]	16.07.42	18.12.44	79	843.6	**79/843.6**
FK194:	206 Sqn [M]	21.08.42	02.07.43	6	39.3	
	220 Sqn	06.08.43	09.09.43	-	-	
	251 Sqn	30.05.45	28.07.45	-	-	**6/48.0**
FK195:	206 Sqn [L]	19.08.42	09.09.43	18	173.5	**18/173.5**
FK196:	220 Sqn [C]	13.07.42	30.08.43	-	-	
	1 OTU	30.08.43	?	-	-	
	1674 HCU	?	22.03.44	-	-	
	519 Sqn	06.01.45	23.03.45	-	-	
	251 Sqn	01.04.45	28.07.45	7	55.1	**7/55.1**
FK197:	251 Sqn [AD-E]	03.05.45	30.07.45	8	61.4	**8/61.4**
FK198:	59 Sqn [M]	09.01.43	08.04.43	2	18.2	
	206 Sqn [W]	15.08.43	19.03.44	9	103.2	
	220 Sqn [R]	19.03.44	19.04.44	4	48.3	**15/169.7**
FK199:	220 Sqn [R]	23.07.42	31.08.43	58	521.1	
	1 OTU	31.08.43	26.10.43	-	-	
	1674 HCU	26.10.43	09.01.44	-	-	
	206 Sqn	09.03.44	31.03.44	-	-	
	220 Sqn [L]	22.08.44	25.11.44	5	61.9	**63/583.0**
FK200:	220 Sqn [B]	11.07.42	25.04.43	37	332.0	
	220 Sqn [B]	30.08.43	06.04.45	22	224.7	**59/556.7**
FK201:	220 Sqn [T]	23.09.42	02.08.43	36	345.5	
	1674 HCU	25.12.43	22.06.45	-	-	**36/345.5**
FK202:	59 Sqn [B]	13.12.42	24.04.43	9	96.3	
	220 Sqn [L]	04.08.43	25.10.43	2	10.4*	**11/106.7***
FK203:	220 Sqn [M]	25.07.42	12.09.43	69	664.2	
	251 Sqn	19.05.45	22.12.45	9	90.4	**78/754.6**
FK204:	220 Sqn [N]	25.07.42	10.10.42	4	20.4*	**4/20.4***
FK205:	59 Sqn [B]	23.01.43	05.02.43	4	31.9	
	59 Sqn [P]	06.02.43	21.04.43	9	98.7	
	1674 HCU [D]	25.12.43	05.09.45	-	-	**13/130.6**
FK206:	220 Sqn [K]	18.07.42	04.12.43	125	736.5*	**125/736.5***
FK207:	220 Sqn [J]	17.07.42	10.08.42	7	51.2	**7/51.2***
FK208:	206 Sqn [B]	04.08.42	29.11.43	57	526.9*	**57/526.9***
FK209:	53 Sqn	13.12.42	31.12.42	-	-	
	59 Sqn [J]	31.12.42	23.03.43	14	146.2*	**14/146.2***
FK210:	206 Sqn [E]	12.08.42	02.07.43	61	577.0	
	220 Sqn [G]	26.10.43	23.12.44	32	317.7	
	519 Sqn [Z9-A]	23.03.45	12.05.45	12	110.8	
	521 Sqn [W]	12.05.45	10.12.45	51	345.0	**156/1350.5**
FK211:	206 Sqn [Z]	03.08.43	31.03.44	24	244.0	
	519 Sqn [Z9-H]	22.01.45	22.09.45	30	262.8	**54/506.8**
FK212:	220 Sqn [V]	31.07.42	14.06.43	54	483.8*	**54/483.8***
FK213:	206 Sqn [C]	04.08.42	19.03.44	90	858.3	
	220 Sqn [L]	19.03.44	22.08.44	2	17.5	
	519 Sqn [Z9-G]	30.12.44	17.09.45	15	153.3	**107/1029.1**
FL449:	220 Sqn [O]	26.08.43	17.11.44	65	695.6	
	519 Sqn [Z9-F]	18.12.44	01.10.45	17	160.8	**82/856.4**
FL450:	59 Sqn [A]	15.12.42	07.04.43	8	88.4	

	Unit	From	To	Ops	Hours	Total
	220 Sqn [U]	07.04.43	30.08.43	16	149.7	
	1 OTU	30.08.43	11.11.43	-	-	
	1674 HCU	11.11.43	14.01.44	-	-	
	519 Sqn [Z9-D]	02.12.44	11.05.45	38	269.1	
	521 Sqn [V]	11.05.45	13.02.45	55	322.5	**117/829.7**
FL451:	206 Sqn [D]	04.08.42	12.09.43	69	639.7	
	206 Sqn	07.03.44	31.03.44	-	-	
	251 Sqn [AD-D]	13.04.45	29.08.45	7	48.0	**76/687.7**
FL452:	206 Sqn [G]	30.07.42	23.10.43	59	575.3	
	206 Sqn [F]	24.10.43	21.11.43	7	75.4	
	521 Sqn [U]	03.02.45	12.02.46	43	276.4	**109/927.1**
FL453:	206 Sqn [A]	30.07.42	14.12.42	27	242.5*	**21/242.5***
FL454:	206 Sqn [J]	15.08.42	06.10.42	3	13.6*	**3/13.6***
FL455:	206 Sqn [N]	12.07.43	31.03.44	31	328.5	
	519 Sqn [Z9-A]	14.11.44	01.02.45	15	140.9	**49/469.4**
FL456:	220 Sqn [N]	20.08.42	12.09.43	88	820.4	
	220 Sqn [N]	18.01.44	04.12.44	33	408.3	
	521 Sqn	22.01.45	25.01.45	36	203.7	**157/1432.4**
FL457:	206 Sqn [F]	30.07.42	08.12.43	56	524.8	
	251 Sqn [AD-P]	02.05.45	29.11.45	12	104.2	
	521 Sqn	29.11.45	18.02.46	3	29.8	**71/658.8**
FL458:	220 Sqn [A]	23.03.43	12.08.43	13	138.6	
	206 Sqn	24.12.43	??.02.44	-	-	
	220 Sqn [Q]	??.02.44	25.11.44	50	557.3	**63/695.9**
FL459:	220 Sqn [J]	20.08.42	18.12.44	83	814.7	
	519 Sqn [Z9-M]	23.03.45	24.07.45	16	131.9	
	251 Sqn [AD-A]	24.07.45	22.12.45	14	113.8	**112/1060.4**
FL460:	206 Sqn [H]	12.08.42	19.03.44	68	670.4	
	220 Sqn [D]	19.03.44	15.12.44	35	420.6	**103/1091.0**
FL461:	not delivered					
FL462:	59 Sqn [C]	31.12.42	07.04.43	9	96	
	220 Sqn [W]	07.04.43	15.09.44	78	801.1	**87/897.1**
FL463:	59 Sqn [D]	31.12.42	21.04.43	9	99.3	
	220 Sqn [D]	21.04.43	17.07.43	-	-	
	1674 HCU	03.02.44	28.09.45	-	-	**9/99.3**
FL464:	59 Sqn [E]	31.12.42	17.04.43	14	148.9	
	220 Sqn [Y]	17.04.43	22.10.43	9	82.3	
	220 Sqn [C]	23.10.43	17.11.44	54	586.9	
	519 Sqn [Z9-B]	09.12.44	01.08.45	46	408.3	
	251 Sqn [AD-E]	01.08.45	22.12.45	5	49.1	**128/1275.5**
HB761:	not delivered					
HB762:	-					
HB763:	214 Sqn [BU-T]	07.06.44	26.08.44	19	85.3*	**19/85.3***
HB764:	not delivered					
HB765:	214 Sqn [BU-R]	30.03.44	10.07.45	62	323.7	**62/323.7**
HB766:	not delivered					
HB767:	214 Sqn [BU-A]	16.06.44	13.09.44	15	71.0*	**15/71.0***
HB768:	-					
HB769:	-					
HB770:	not delivered					
HB771:	not delivered					
HB772:	214 Sqn [BU-Q]	18.07.44	18.08.45	43	196.2	**43/196.2**
HB773:	-					
HB774:	214 Sqn [BU-G]	07.06.44	23.08.45	44	221.1	**44/221.1**
HB775:	-					
HB776:	1674 HCU	16.04.44	28.09.44	-	-	
HB777:	-					
HB778:	1674 HCU	10.05.44	22.10.44	-	-	
HB779:	214 Sqn [BU-K]	??.10.44	21.02.45	33	181.4	
	214 Sqn [BU-P]	24.03.45	23.08.45	3	19.6	**36/201.0**

Serial	Unit	From	To	Ops	Hours	Total
HB780:	214 Sqn [BU-C]	14.07.44	22.08.45	46	222.0	**45/222.0**
HB781:	not delivered					
HB782:	-					
HB783:	not delivered					
HB784:	not delivered					
HB785:	214 Sqn [BU-A]	??.09.44	21.03.45	51	288.7*	**51/288.7***
HB786:	220 Sqn [V]	09.04.44	26.04.45	5	44.4	
	521 Sqn [Q]	09.06.45	04.02.46	66	476.6	**71/521.0**
HB787:	214 Sqn [BU-J]	31.07.44	16.11.44	34	155	**34/155**
HB788:	214 Sqn [BU-B]	10.08.44	06.11.44	29	156.4*	**28/156.4***
HB789:	214 Sqn [BU-Q]	17.01.45	??.08.45	25	146.8	**25/146.8**
HB790:	214 Sqn [BU-Q]	11.12.44	15.01.45	1	6.6	
	214 Sqn	03.05.45	23.08.45	-	-	**1/6.6**
HB791:	220 Sqn [T]	29.06.44	25.03.45	40	498.2	
	251 Sqn [AD-L]	31.08.45	27.12.45	-	-	**40/498.2**
HB792:	220 Sqn [U]	29.06.44	30.03.45	33	427.3	
	251 Sqn [AD-D]	31.08.45	20.12.45	-	-	**33/427.3**
HB793:	214 Sqn [BU-S]	16.08.44	25.04.45	63	317.7	
	1699 Flt [4Z-S]	25.04.45	13.06.45	-	-	
	223 Sqn [6G-Q]	13.06.45	24.08.45	-	-	**63/317.7**
HB794:	not delivered					
HB795:	214 Sqn [BU-N]	30.09.44	21.03.45	1	4.4	**1/4.4**
HB796:	214 Sqn [BU-T]	06.09.44	08.02.45	43	210.8*	**41/210.8***
HB797:	not delivered					
HB798:	not delivered					
HB799:	214 Sqn [BU-K in Feb.45]	09.09.44	14.04.45	5	30.9	
	214 Sqn [BU-L]	??	23.08.45	1	5.1	**6/36.0**
HB800:	214 Sqn [BU-V]	09.09.44	31.10.44	8	41.5	**8/41.5**
HB801:	214 Sqn [BU-U]	24.08.44	18.12.44	38	174.8	
	214 Sqn [BU-T]	09.02.45	18.08.45	16	94.5	**54/269.3**
HB802:	214 Sqn [BU-O]	16.08.44	14.03.45	58	282.5*	**58/282.5***
HB803:	214 Sqn [BU-L]	23.08.44	15.03.45	67	349.3*	**67/349.3***
HB804:	not delivered					
HB805:	214 Sqn [BU-C]	14.01.45	24.02.45	6	32.2*	**6/32.2***
HB806:	not delivered					
HB807:	not delivered					
HB808:	not delivered					
HB809:	not delivered					
HB810:	not delivered					
HB811:	not delivered					
HB812:	not delivered					
HB813:	not delivered					
HB814:	not delivered					
HB815:	214 Sqn [BU-J]	08.12.44	04.03.45	30	171.5*	**30/171.5***
HB816:	214 Sqn [BU-F]	09.12.44	22.08.45	37	215.2	**37/215.2**
HB817:	214 Sqn [BU-G]	16.03.45	22.08.45	12	103.6	**12/103.6**
HB818:	214 Sqn [BU-H]	30.09.44	07.03.45	25	127.9	
	1699 Flt	07.03.45	13.06.45	-	-	
	223 Sqn	13.06.45	?	-	-	**25/127.9**
HB819:	214 Sqn [BU-U]	14.01.45	18.08.45	20	121.7	**20/121.7**
HB820:	214 Sqn [BU-P]	30.11.44	14.02.45	7	34.2	**7/34.2**
KH998:	223 Sqn [6G-C]	20.04.45	26.07.45	1	5.0	**1/5.0**
KH999:	214 Sqn [BU-M]	15.01.45	17.08.45	26	182.1	**26/182.1**
KJ100:	223 Sqn	21.06.45	09.08.45	-	-	
	RWE	09.08.45	20.10.45	-	-	
KJ101:	214 Sqn [BU-H]	20.03.45	23.08.45	5	29.0	**5/29.0**
KJ102:	223 Sqn	28.04.45	09.08.45	-	-	
	RWE	09.08.45	20.10.45	-	-	
KJ103:	214 Sqn [BU-M]	09.12.44	16.01.45	13	76.6*	**13/76.6***
KJ104:	214 Sqn [BU-D]	28.11.44	25.04.45	35	203.0	

	1699 Flt	25.04.45	13.06.45	-	-	
	223 Sqn	13.06.45	24.08.45	-	-	**35/203.0**
KJ105:	223 Sqn	01.05.45	09.08.45	-	-	
	RWE	09.08.45	20.10.45	-	-	-
KJ106:	214 Sqn [BU-G]	31.12.44	07.03.45	10	49.6*	**10/49.6***
KJ107:	214 Sqn [BU-N]	09.12.44	14.08.45	31	196.5	**31/196.5**
KJ108:	-	-	-	-	-	
KJ109:	214 Sqn [BU-V]	11.12.44	25.04.45	8	50.1	
	1699 Flt	25.04.45	13.06.45	-	-	
	223 Sqn [6G-F]	13.06.45	24.08.45	-	-	**8/50.1**
KJ110:	214 Sqn [BU-B]	28.11.44	04.06.45	18	103.4	
	223 Sqn [6G-P]	04.06.45	25.08.45	-	-	**18/103.4**
KJ111:	214 Sqn [BU-C]	26.02.45	22.08.45	9	53.8	**9/53.8**
KJ112:	214 Sqn [BU-P]	26.02.45	22.03.45	1	?	**1/?**
KJ113:	223 Sqn [6G-D]	21.04.45	09.08.45	1	4.6	**1/4.6**
	RWE	09.08.45	20.10.45	-	-	
KJ114:	214 Sqn [BU-B]	07.02.45	22.08.45	11	56.9	**11/56.9**
KJ115:	223 Sqn	21.04.45	09.08.45	-	-	
	RWE	09.08.45	20.10.45	-	-	
KJ116:	-	-	-	-	-	
KJ117:	223 Sqn [6G-E]	28.04.45	09.08.45	-	-	
	RWE [3U-E]	09.08.45	20.10.45	-	-	
KJ118:	214 Sqn	05.04.45	16.04.45	-	-	
	223 Sqn [6G-H]	16.04.45	09.08.45	4	16.5	
	RWE	09.08.45	20.10.45	-	-	**4/16.5**
KJ119:	214 Sqn [BU-O]	20.03.45	14.08.45	6	41.0	**6/41.0**
KJ120:	223 Sqn	23.04.45	09.08.45	-	-	
	RWE	09.08.45	20.10.45	-	-	

KJ118 with its serials painted in white under the wings as the regulations stipulated from the summer of 1945 onwards. Its former codes of the RWE have been painted over which is not the case for the other two Fortresses on.

KJ121:	214 Sqn	11.04.45	16.04.45	-	-	
	223 Sqn [6G-B]	16.04.45	24.08.45	4	18.6	**4/18.6**
KJ122:	214 Sqn [BU-D]	30.03.45	22.08.45	1	4.8	**1/4.8**
KJ123:	-	-	-	-	-	
KJ124:	223 Sqn	29.04.45	25.08.45	-	-	
KJ125:	214 Sqn [BU-J]	07.03.45	17.04.45	5	34.8	**5/34.8**
KJ126:	-	-	-	-	-	
KJ127:	-	-	-	-	-	
KL830:	-	-	-	-	-	
KL831:	-	-	-	-	-	
KL832:	-	-	-	-	-	
KL833:	-	-	-	-	-	
KL834:	-	-	-	-	-	
KL835:	-	-	-	-	-	
KL836:	-	-	-	-	-	
KL837:	-	-	-	-	-	
SR376:	214 Sqn [BU-C]	02.02.44	08.12.44	-	-	
	1699 Flt	08.12.44	31.12.44	-	-	-
SR377:	214 Sqn [BU-M]	29.01.44	09.02.45	30	106.6	**30/106.6**
SR378:	214 Sqn [BU-D]	02.02.44	04.01.45	30	106.6	**30/106.6**
SR379:	214 Sqn [BU-O]	03.02.44	31.12.44	10	28.8	**10/28.8**
SR380:	214 Sqn [BU-S]	02.02.44	17.08.44	11	24.8	
	1699 Flt [4Z-Y]**	17.08.44	19.10.44	2	6.2	**13/31.0**
SR381:	214 Sqn [BU-F]	02.02.44	22.06.44	19	71.7	**19/71.7**
SR382:	214 Sqn [BU-B]	02.02.44	22.06.44	18	67.0*	**18/67.0***
SR383:	214 Sqn [BU-F]	29.01.44	??.09.44	21	89.3	
	214 Sqn [BU-X]	??.09.44	08.12.44	1	3.9	
	1699 Flt [4Z-X]	08.12.44	04.07.45	-	-	**22/93.2**
SR384:	214 Sqn [BU-A]	02.02.44	25.05.44	14	51.2*	**14/51.2***
SR385:	214 Sqn [BU-E]	02.02.44	30.08.45	-	-	-
SR386:	214 Sqn [BU-N]	28.01.44	08.12.44	31	137.6	
	1699 Flt [4Z-Y]**	08.12.44	12.05.45	4	17.3	**35/154.9**
SR387:	214 Sqn [BU-G]	02.02.44	14.02.45	-	-	-
SR388:	214 Sqn [BU-H]	02.02.44	08.12.44	34	134.0	
	1699 Flt [4Z-Z]**	08.12.44	04.07.45	5	24.4	**39/158.4**
SR389:	214 Sqn [BU-P]	05.02.44	07.01.45	14	42.7	**14/42.7**

Note: A number of sorties cannot be identified, 7 for the 214, 1 for the 519 (aircraft coded 'S'), 2 for the 521.
*Aircraft lost on operation, total of hours calculated from the last return recorded.
**To be confirmed

Fourth from left, Flight Lieutenant G.H. Bremness (RCAF) posing with his crew in front of KJ121/6G-B with which he flew four sorties at the end of the war.

IN MEMORIAM
Boeing Fortress Mk. II & III

Name	Service No	Rank	Age	Origin	Date	Serial
Abbott, Norman William Stanley	RAF No. 1626469	Sgt	n/k	RAF	22.06.44	SR382
Allan, Kenneth Cecil	RAF No. 183538	F/O	n/k	RAF	24.02.45	HB805
Allies, William Donald	RAF No. 41978	F/L	30	RAF	22.02.45	KJ112
Armstrong, Ernest Robert	NZ427084	F/Sgt	20	RNZAF	16.11.44	HB787
Arnold, William James	Can./ R.106166	W/O II	20	RCAF	23.03.43	FK209
Ashworth, Colin James	NZ427492	F/Sgt	22	RNZAF	16.11.44	HB787
Banner, William Taylor	RAF No. 2221107	Sgt	37	RAF	09.02.45	HB796
Barnfield, Harry	RAF No. 1059973	F/Sgt	24	RAF	04.03.45	HB815
Beatson, Alexander Purdie	AAF No. 823239	Sgt	n/k	RAF	01.02.45	FL455
Bennett, Harry	RAF No. 190245	F/O	24	RAF	04.03.45	HB815
Bennett, Lionel John	NZ42287	W/O	25	RNZAF	09.02.45	HB796
Benson, George Henry	RAF No. 989053	Sgt	23	RAF	12.09.44	HB767
Bentley, Rupert	RAF No. 1115124	Sgt	32	RAF	14.12.42	FL453
Billington, Leslie Ernest	RAF No. 2205644	Sgt	20	RAF	04.03.45	HB815
Billington, Thomas Hornby	RAF No. 1044838	Sgt	22	RAF	12.09.44	HB767
Birky, Ronnie	RAF No. 1549729	Sgt	22	RAF	12.09.44	HB767
Boag, George	RAF No. 1554282	F/Sgt	23	RAF	26.08.44	HB763
Boudreault, Joseph Edouard Roch	Can./ R.125388	W/O II	22	RCAF	04.12.43	FK206
Braithwaite, Charles Roberts William	RAF No. 1812034	F/Sgt	n/k	RAF	22.03.45	KJ112
Briddon, William	RAF No. 1817057	F/Sgt	27	RAF	04.03.45	HB815
Bristow, Ernest William	RAF No. 745118	W/O	26	RAF	10.08.42	FK207
Brown, David Thomas	RAF No. 3031563	Sgt	20	RAF	08.01.46	FA703
Brown, Donald Brooke	RAF No. 1066461	W/O	22	RAF	29.11.43	FK208
Brown, Ralph	RAF No. 78250	S/L	33	RAF	06.01.44	FA705
Bryant, Sydney Herbert	RAF No.1821276	Sgt	20	RAF	22.06.44	SR382
Buckland, Peter George	RAF No. 1337316	F/Sgt	n/k	RAF	09.02.45	HB796
Burnett, Robert Alfred Charles	RAF No. 1270447	F/Sgt	21	RAF	29.11.43	FK208
Bunyan, William	RAF No. 1118147	Sgt	35	RAF	09.02.45	HB796
Caldwell, Donald Forest	Can./ J.11098	F/L	32	RCAF	04.11.45	9202
Callender, Charles Francis	RAF No. 68777	F/L	36	RAF	14.06.43	FK212
Campion, Michael Patrick	RAF No. 536451	W/O	27	RAF	04.12.43	FK206
Capel, David Farquhar	Aus. 404602	P/O	22	RAAF	10.08.42	FK207
Carrott, Robert James	RAF No. 1816917	Sgt	20	RAF	09.02.45	HB796
Carter, Hilton Mackay	Can./ J.94203	P/O	22	RCAF	21.03.45	HB785
Cassan, John Douglas	RAF No. 172119	P/O	21	RAF	22.06.44	SR382
Cathcart, Norman Carel	Can./ C.6248	F/O	n/k	(us)/RCAF	02.04.44	9207
Caulfield, Gordon John Joseph	RAF No. 1895558	Sgt	23	RAF	26.08.44	HB763
Christie, Alexander Baxter	RAF No. 1375581	F/Sgt	29	RAF	25.10.43	FK202
Cojocar, George	Can./ J.16374	P/O	22	RCAF	23.03.43	FK209
Comba, William Minor	Can./ R.59670	W/O I	22	RCAF	14.06.43	FK212
Cooper, Norman	RAF No. 916151	W/O	29	RAF	22.03.45	KJ112
Copping, Clarence Lummis	Can./ R.77233	W/O II	25	RCAF	23.03.43	FK209
Coutts, David Strang	RAF No. 1023023	W/O	29	RAF	29.11.43	FK208

Crowe, Eric	RAF No. 964953	F/Sgt	25	RAF	14.12.42	FL453
Cryer, Jacques Edward	RAF No. 141282	F/L	23	RAF	15.03.45	HB803
Cummings, Reginald George	RAF No. 56649	F/O	24	RAF	08.01.46	FA703
Cunningham, Wilfred James	RAF No. 149252	F/O	24	RAF	22.03.45	KJ112
Dack, Kenneth Peter	RAF No. 154246	F/O	20	RAF	12.09.44	HB767
Dale, William Denis	RAF No. 1594366	Sgt	n/k	RAF	21.03.45	HB785
Davison, George	RAF No. 989245	Sgt	22	RAF	14.06.43	FK212
Day, Kenneth Anthony Ian	RAF No. 1234239	F/Sgt	26	RAF	01.02.45	FL455
Delarue, Jack Edmond	Aus. 402322	F/O	26	RAAF	06.10.42	FL454
Dickson, Cecil Alexander	Can./ J.10870	F/O	24	RCAF	15.12.44	9203
Dix, Francis Herbert	NZ411069	W/O	24	RNZAF	24.02.45	HB805
Dobson, Edwin	RAF No. 1442409	Sgt	n/k	RAF	12.09.44	HB767
Dobson, Ernest	RAF No. 1590215	Sgt	20	RAF	09.02.45	HB796
Dodds, Robert Leslie	RAF No. 172519	P/O	n/k	RAF	12.09.44	HB767
Donald, Douglas Nogent	Can./ J.47071	F/O	23	(US)/RCAF	21.03.45	HB785
Duncan, Joseph Henry	RAF No. 126994	F/O	24	RAF	06.01.44	FA705
Dungate, Alfred William	Can./ J.16441	F/O	24	RCAF	25.10.43	FK202
Dunn, Denis Macrorie	RAF No. 141755	P/O	30	RAF	26.03.43	FA698
Durman, Peter Edward	RAF No. 1389300	Sgt	n/k	RAF	16.11.44	HB787
Eckersley, Thomas	RAF No. 1533557	F/Sgt	31	RAF	06.01.44	FA705
Fabian, Robert	RAF No. 1288265	Sgt	24	RAF	06.01.44	FA705
Fage, Jeffrey	RAF No. 1172715	Sgt	23	RAF	26.03.43	FA698
Filleul, Philip Richard Steuart	RAF No. 33383	F/L	26	RAF	12.09.44	HB767
Flack, Carl Thomas	Can./ R.121119	W/O II	23	RCAF	04.12.43	FK206
Foster, Philip Gerard	RAF No. 1158929	Sgt	21	RAF	10.08.42	FK207
Fowler, George Swan Murray	Aus. 442340	F/Sgt	19	RAAF	09.02.45	HB796
Fowler, Leslie Gordon	RAF No. 126036	F/L	23	RAF	15.03.45	HB805
Fretter, Victor Clarence	RAF No. 751381	Sgt	23	RAF	10.08.42	FK207
Frost, Harold**	RAF No. 169864	F/O	24	RAF	17.03.45	HB799
Frost, Shadrach Morton	RAF No. 1379682	Sgt	30	RAF	14.06.43	FK212
Garcia, Harry	RAF No. 931532	Sgt	20	RAF	10.08.42	FK207
Gaunt, Gordon Thomas	Can./ J.14910	F/O	25	RCAF	02.04.44	9207
Guppy, John Flower	Aus. 406452	Sgt	20	RAAF	06.10.42	FL454
Hader, Leslie	RAF No. 1804649	F/Sgt	20	RAF	04.03.45	HB815
Hall, Gordon Albert**	RAF No. 149916	F/O	22	RAF	17.03.45	HB799
Hanet, Jean-Pierre	RAF No. 1819763	Sgt	n/k	RAF	12.09.44	HB767
Harbidge, James William	RAF No. 1220213	F/Sgt	32	RAF	14.06.43	FK212
Hares, Frank	RAF No. 1581827	F/Sgt	21	RAF	04.03.45	HB815
Harling, Edward Patrick	Can./ J.4331	F/L	28	RCAF	04.11.45	9202
Healy, Patrick James	RAF No. 1300369	Sgt	24	RAF	04.03.45	HB815
Heard, Donald Luther	Can./ R.105458	W/O I	35	RCAF	06.01.44	FA705
Henderson, Harry Leonard	Can./ J.95282	P/O	19	RCAF	07.03.45	KJ106
Hildred, Robert Nockold	RAF No. 1333535	Sgt	21	RAF	14.12.42	FL453
Hillcoat, Horace Brougham	Can./ C.21305	F/L	31	RCAF	15.12.44	9203
Hislop, Gilbert Leslie	RAF No. 1594952	F/Sgt	32	RAF	16.11.44	HB787
Hockley, Allan James Neville	Aus. 420197	P/O	27	RAAF	25.05.44	SR384
Jaeger, James Cleveland Harold Rudolf	RAF No. 1382407	Sgt	31	RAF	06.10.42	FL454
Johnson, James Geoffrey	Aus. 408252	P/O	20	RAAF	04.12.43	FK206
Jones, Allan Milton	RAF No. 178636	F/O	n/k	RAF	24.02.45	HB805
Jones, Robert Alan Derek	RAF No. 1811322	Sgt	20	RAF	22.03.45	KJ112
Jones, Stanley Llewellyn	RAF No. 1256275	F/Sgt	n/k	RAF	24.02.45	HB805
Keddy, Oliver Ambrose	Can./ R.88434	W/O I	24	RCAF	06.01.44	FA706
Kerr, Brian Francis	RAF No. 148842	F/O	n/k	RAF	22.03.45	KJ112
Kingdon, Robert Verdun	Can./ J.28299	F/O	28	RCAF	21.03.45	HB785
La Brish, Frederick Blair	Can. /J. 4763	F/L	n/k	RCAF	15.12.44	9203
Lavergne, Elmer Ivan	Can./ R.156555	Cpl	n/k	RCAF	02.04.44	9207
Lawson, Harold	RAF No. 149162	P/O	23	RAF	04.12.43	FK206

Leitch, Archibald Havill	Can./ J.44328	F/O	21	RCAF	16.11.44	HB787
Matthews, Sidney Claiden**	RAF No. 142217	F/L	25	RAF	17.03.45	HB799
McClymont, Hugh Mcclure	RAF No. 1681945	F/Sgt	n/k	RAF	07.03.45	KJ106
McCormack, Terence Francis	NZ429183	F/Sgt	24	RNZAF	16.11.44	HB787
McFadden, Hugh Charles	Can./ J.14632	F/O	30	RCAF	02.04.44	9207
McFarlane, James	RAF No. 994024	W/O	23	RAF	22.03.45	KJ112
McKay, John Smith	RAF No. 1325202	F/Sgt	27	RAF	25.10.43	FK202
McKee, Terrance Velleau	Can./ J.37716	F/O	24	RCAF	17.01.45	KJ103
McLaren, William Alistair	RAF No. 1672260	F/Sgt	21	RAF	16.11.44	HB787
McLaughlin, Alexander	NZ422972	F/Sgt	27	RNZAF	16.11.44	HB787
McNamara, Anthony John	RAF No. 1582886	Sgt	n/k	RAF	26.08.44	HB763
Micthener, Denis John Anthony	RAF No. 1450109	F/Sgt	21	RAF	29.11.43	FK208
Miller, Donald Fraser	RAF No. 1809260	F/Sgt	n/k	RAF	21.03.45	HB785
Montgomery, Richard Glover	Can./ R.106426	W/O II	26	RCAF	23.03.43	FK209
Mooney, Richard Edmond	Can./ R.261225	Sgt	31	RCAF	16.11.44	HB787
Morris, Desmond Edward	RAF No. 132320	F/O	n/k	RAF	04.12.43	FK206
Morrison, Robert Noel	RAF No. 1192004	F/Sgt	22	RAF	04.12.43	FK206
Moule, Arthur Edward	RAF No. 126145	F/O	24	RAF	29.11.43	FK208
Newark, Edgar Stanley	RAF No. 1331073	W/O	25	RAF	08.01.46	FA703
Newman, Peter	RAF No. 1816804	Sgt	n/k	RAF	22.03.45	KJ112
Odgers, Lindsay Joseph	Aus. 417595	W/O	21	RAAF	04.03.45	HB815
Offler, William Henry	Can./ J.22508	F/O	33	RCAF	24.10.43	FK202
Ogilvie, Charles Gordon Mackay	RAF No. 621667	Sgt	28	RAF	16.11.44	HB787
Olds, Frederick Rossini	NZ427313	F/Sgt	31	RNZAF	09.02.45	HB796
Orr, George	RAF No. 1551656	F/Sgt	21	RAF	22.06.44	SR382
Owen, John	RAF No. 63800	F/O	21	RAF	14.12.42	FL453
Paddick, Ernest George	RAF No. 179426	F/O	23	RAF	08.02.45	KJ110*
Panzer, Geoffrey Arthur Francis	RAF No. 1384480	F/Sgt	21	RAF	01.02.45	FL455
Parnell, William James	RAF No. 1163993	Sgt	22	RAF	14.12.42	FL453
Patterson, George Scaife	RAF No. 1051252	Sgt	23	RAF	14.06.43	FK212
Payne, William Henry	RAF No. 1738660	F/Sgt	20	RAF	01.02.45	FL455
Pearce, Arthur	Aus. 406868	P/O	25	RAAF	04.12.43	FK206
Pellant, James Walter	Can./ J.95470	P/O	21	RCAF	21.03.45	HB785
Percival, Edward Arthur**	RAF No. 1263001	F/Sgt	30	RAF	17.03.45	HB799
Perkins, Walter	RAF No. 2223326	Sgt	19	RAF	21.03.45	HB785
Peters, Nicholas	Can./ J.45525	F/O	30	RCAF	07.03.45	KJ106
Phillips, Edwin Erwin	Can./ R.174196	Sgt	24	RCAF	04.11.45	9202
Phillips, Robert Albert	RAF No. 128609	F/O	31	RAF	23.03.43	FK209
Pinhorn, Anthony James	RAF No. 42468	S/L	28	(can)/RAF	06.01.44	FA705
Pollard, Thomas William James	RAF No. 1865782	F/Sgt	19	RAF	24.02.45	HB805
Potter, William Thomas	RAF No. 143930	P/O	30	RAF	25.10.43	FK202
Pressley, Dennis Alfred	RAF No. 1640545	Sgt	21	RAF	01.02.45	FL455
Probst, Charles Percival	RAF No. 979949	F/Sgt	33	RAF	14.06.43	FK212
Punnett, Edward Lionel	RAF No. 1606932	Sgt	n/k	RAF	22.03.45	KJ112
Roberts, Francis Dennis	RAF No. 122972	F/O	34	RAF	06.01.44	FA705
Robertson, James Peter	NZ422318	P/O	23	RNZAF	09.02.45	HB796
Robinson, Frederick Arthur	RAF No. 1376615	F/Sgt	29	RAF	06.10.42	FL454
Roche, Norbert	Can./J. 15269	F/L	28	RCAF	04.11.45	9202
Routley, William Arthur	Can./ J.9326	P/O	31	RCAF	21.03.45	HB785
Ruttledge, Alfred John de Laune	Can./ J.15160	F/L	30	RCAF	15.12.44	9203
Sandelin, Robert Simeon	Can./ R.82680	W/O II	24	RCAF	26.03.43	FA698
Sanderson, Gordon Alan	RAF No. 128370	P/O	23	RAF	10.08.42	FK207
Senior, Ronald Andrew	RAF No. 1115843	Sgt	23	RAF	29.11.43	FK208
Shanahan, John Donald	Can./ J.16166	F/O	n/k	(us)/RCAF	02.04.44	9207
Shanks, Walter	RAF No. 1067932	Sgt	21	RAF	14.12.42	FL453
Sharp, George Boyd	RAF No. 164868	F/O	23	RAF	08.01.46	FA703
Sharpe, Alex	RAF No. 1011102	F/Sgt	23	RAF	22.06.44	SR382

59

Shortlle, Joseph Malpass	RAF No. 157422	F/O	27	RAF	24.02.45	HB805
Simpson, Raymond George Victor	RAF No. 1805752	Sgt	20	RAF	25.05.44	SR384
Sinclair, Stafford Henry George	RAF No. 178092	F/O	32	RAF	22.03.45	KJ112
Spino, Frank	Can./ R.75875	W/O II	26	RCAF	23.03.43	FK209
Stares, Ronald Norman	RAF No. 931486	W/O	25	RAF	06.01.44	FA705
Stewart, George	NZ421849	F/O	22	RNZAF	07.03.45	KJ106
Stones, James	RAF No. 751932	F/Sgt	23	RAF	29.11.43	FK208
Taplin, John Batch	Aus. 407607	F/Sgt	27	RAAF	06.10.42	FL454
Towell, Richard William	RAF No. 195111	P/O	30	RAF	24.02.45	HB805
Thrower, James Kendel	RAF No. 1435458	F/Sgt	n/k	RAF	08.01.46	FA703
Usher, Thomas Wilfred Henry	RAF No. 3050447	Sgt	20	RAF	09.02.45	HB796
Varney, Maxwell Everette	Can./ R.71569	W/O I	24	RCAF	25.10.43	FK202
Verney, James Way	RAF No. 80395	F/O	30	(SA)/RAF	14.06.43	FK212
Vinall, James William **	RAF No. 169518	F/O	40	RAF	17.03.45	HB799
Walton, James	RAF No. 131472	F/O	n/k	RAF	25.10.43	FK202
Weatherhead, Richard John	Can./ J.6992	F/O	30	RCAF	23.03.43	FK209
Webster, Alfred Ernest	Can./ J.4956	S/L	36	RCAF	04.11.45	9202
Webster, Harry Argur Andrew	RAF No. 37619	S/L	28	RAF	25.10.43	FK202
White, Maurice Charles	RAF No. 1166191	W/O	25	RAF	15.05.45	HB803
Williamson, Donald	RAF No. 1777442	Sgt	21	RAF	26.08.44	HB763
Wilson, Garfield Charles	NZ411113	Sgt	21	RNZAF	14.12.42	FL453
Wilson, John	RAF No. 1120348	F/Sgt	n/k	RAF	29.11.43	FK208
Wilson, Patrick John	RAF No. 1806740	Sgt	31	RAF	12.09.44	HB767
Wilson, Robert George	Can./ R.197780	W/O II	21	RCAF	21.03.45	HB785
Winstone, John William	NZ429389	P/O	25	RNZAF	07.03.45	KJ106
Wood, Edwin Arthur	RAF No. 109926	F/L	24	RAF	12.02.45	FL455
Woodger, Frank Richard	RAF No. 52114	F/L	32	RAF	24.02.45	HB805
Wright, Edward	RAF No. 978768	F/Sgt	22	RAF	14.06.43	FK212
Zapfe, William Christian	Can./ J.7024	F/O	27	RCAF	23.03.43	FK209

*Killed on baord but aircraft returned safely
**Murdered after bailing out over enemy-held territory while the aircraft returned safely to base.

Total: 186

Australia: 9, Canada: 39, New Zealand: 11, South Africa: 1, United Kigdom: 123, USA: 3

n/k: not known

The crew of Fortress SR384/BU-A, the first Fortress lost by 214 Sqn. It was captained by Pilot Officer Allan Hockley (RAAF), seated and third form left. He was killed with the loss of SR384 with Sergeant Ray Simpson, just behind Hockley while the rest of the crew was taken into captivity until the ned of the war. *(214 Sqn Association)*

Boeing Fortress Mk.IIA FK202
No. 59 Squadron
Thorney Island (UK), January 1943

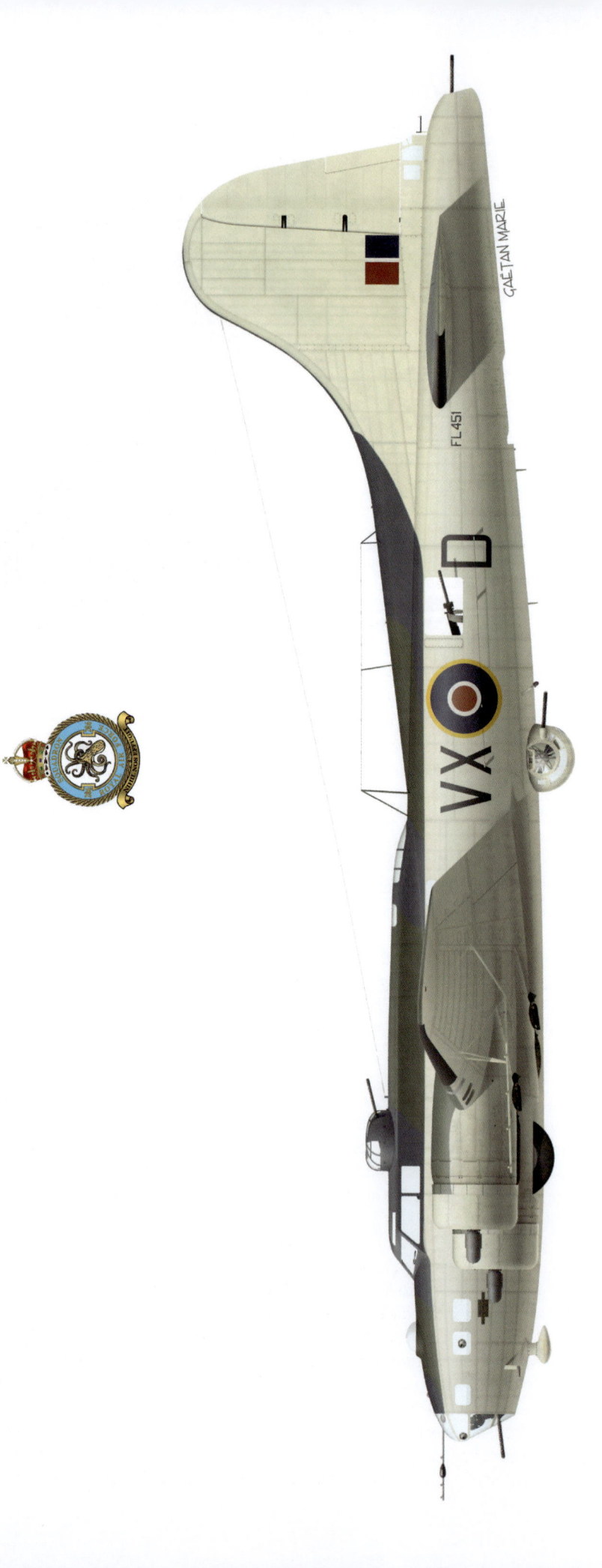

Boeing Fortress Mk. IIA FL451
No. 206 Squadron
Benbecula (UK), Autumn 1942

Boeing Fortress Mk.II FA704
No. 206 Squadron
Benbecula (UK), June 1943

Boeing Fortress B.III KJ117
No. 223 Squadron
Oulton (UK), May 1945

Boeing Fortress Mk.IIA FL464
No. 220 Squadron
Lagens (Azores), 1943 - 1944

Boeing Fortress Mk.II FA696
No. 251 Squadron
Reykjavik (Iceland), Summer 1945

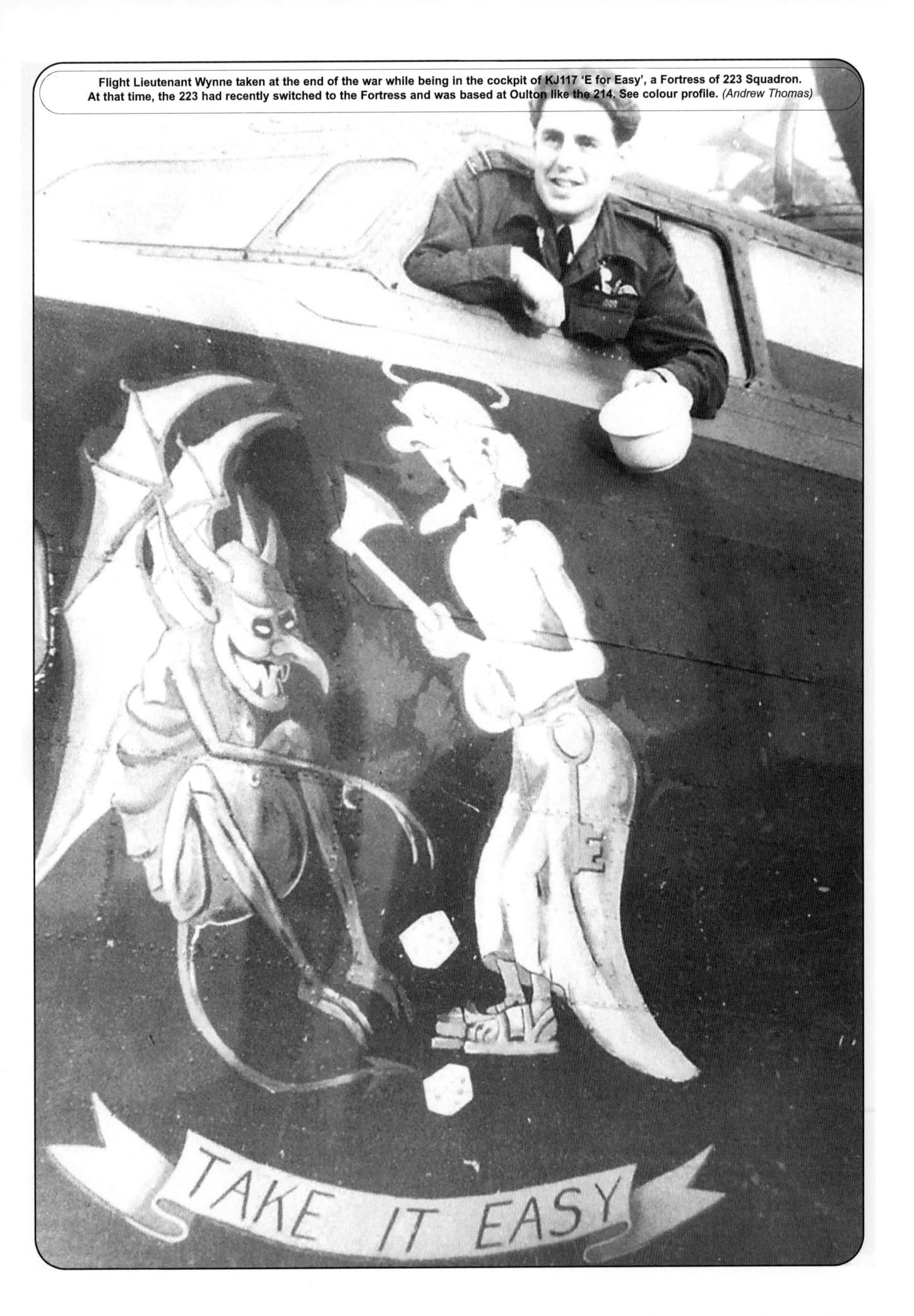

Flight Lieutenant Wynne taken at the end of the war while being in the cockpit of KJ117 'E for Easy', a Fortress of 223 Squadron. At that time, the 223 had recently switched to the Fortress and was based at Oulton like the 214. See colour profile. *(Andrew Thomas)*

TAKE IT EASY

SQUADRONS! - The series

1. The Supermarine Spitfire Mk VI
2. The Republic Thunderbolt Mk I
3. The Supermarine Spitfire Mk V in the Far East
4. The Boeing Fortress Mk I
5. The Supermarine Spitfire Mk XII
6. The Supermarine Spitfire Mk VII
7. The Supermarine Spitfire F. 21
8. The Handley-Page Halifax Mk I
9. The Forgotten Fighters
10. The NA Mustang IV in Western Europe
11. The NA Mustang IV over the Balkans and Italy
12. The Supermarine Spitfire Mk XVI - The British
13. The Martin Marauder Mk I
14. The Supermarine Spitfire Mk VIII - The British
15. The Gloster Meteor F.I & F.III
16. The NA Mitchell - The Dutch, Poles and French
17. The Curtiss Mohawk
18. The Curtiss Kittyhawk Mk II
19. The Boulton Paul Defiant - day and night fighter
20. The Supermarine Spitfire Mk VIII - The Australians
21. The Boeing Fortress Mk II & Mk III
22. The Douglas Boston and Havoc - The Australians
23. The Republic Thunderbolt Mk II
24. The Douglas Boston and Havoc - Night fighters
25. The Supermarine Spitfire Mk V - The Eagles
26. The Hawker Hurricane - The Canadians
27. The Supermarine Spitfire Mk V - The 'Bombay' squadrons
28. The Consolidated Liberator - The Australians
29. The Supermarine Spitfire Mk XVI - The Dominions
30. The Supermarine Spitfire Mk V - The Belgian and Dutch squadrons
31. The Supermarine Spitfire Mk V - The New Zealanders
32. The Supermarine Spitfire Mk V - The Norwegians
33. The Brewster Buffalo
34. The Supermarine Spitfire Mk II - The Foreign squadrons
35. The Martin Marauder Mk II
36. The Supermarine Spitfire Mk V - The Special Reserve squadrons
37. The Supermarine Spitfire Mk XIV - The Belgian and Dutch squadrons
38. The Supermarine Spitfire Mk II - The Rhodesian, Dominion & Eagle squadrons
39. The Douglas Boston and Havoc - Intruders
40. The North American Mustang Mk III over Italy and the Balkans (Pt-1)
41. The Bristol Brigand
42. The Supermarine Spitfire Mk V - The Australians
43. The Hawker Typhoon - The Rhodesian squadrons
44. The Supermarine Spitfire F.22 & F.24
45. The Supermarine Spitfire Mk IX - The Belgian and Dutch squadrons
46. The North American & CAC Mustang - The RAAF
47. The Westland Whirlwind
48. The Supermarine Spitfire Mk XIV - The British squadrons
49. The Supermarine Spitfire Mk I - The beginning (the Auxiliary squadrons)
50. The Hawker Tempest Mk V - The New Zealanders
51. The Last of the Long-Range Biplane Flying Boats
52. The Supermarine Spitfire Mk IX - The Former Canadian Homefront squadrons
53. The Hawker Hurricane Mk I & Mk II - The Eagle Squadrons
54. The Hawker biplane fighters

www.RAF-IN-COMBAT.com

- USN Aircraft 1922-1962 -
- Squadrons! -
- RAF, Dominion and Allied squadrons at War -
- Allied Wings -
- Famous squadrons of WW2 -
- Fighter Leaders -

Printed by Amazon Italia Logistica S.r.l.
Torrazza Piemonte (TO), Italy